A COUNTRY BOY REMINISCES

A Memoir

Keith Wood

authorHOUSE®

AuthorHouse™
1663 Liberty Drive
Bloomington, IN 47403
www.authorhouse.com
Phone: 1 (800) 839-8640

Published by AuthorHouse 08/06/2018

ISBN: 978-1-5462-5383-9 (sc)
ISBN: 978-1-5462-5382-2 (e)

Dedicated to Arden and Norma Jean Wood,
who committed themselves to their family,
their farm, their church, and their God.

Table of Contents

Acknowledgments

I need to thank my high school classmate, Valinda Chafa Johnson, who authored her book, "In My Father's House Again" in 2011. Her efforts caused me to awaken one morning in early March, 2018, desiring to record my version of Wood family history in a memoir.

I extend my thanks to my wife Doris for correcting every page as it was written. I did not realize how many mistakes I made when writing.

Many family members and friends got to read pertinent chapters as I progressed. Thank you for your comments and encouragement.

Several friends and family edited the manuscript as it came closer to the publishing stage. Thank you Mike and Ruth Senneff, Mary and Marvin Wood, Cheryl and Tim Headley, Steve Thomsen, Carol Davis, Pam O'Briant, Janine Sunderman, Joyce Weinkauf, Marc and Kelley Wood, Kamryn Wood, and Doris Wood.

Steve Thomsen helped me organize and send the manuscript and pictures to Authorhouse. My lack of computer savy made someone like Steve necessary. In fact you probably would have had to look at hand-drawn stick men if Steve had not organized and cropped these pictures for me.

Finally, thanks to the eight close family members, who contributed to the index, adding their insights into the Wood family they know.

×

Preface

The five main reasons I took on this writing challenge.

<u>Number one</u>, I wanted to honor my parents and grandparents for a life well lived. They committed their lives to people and ideas bigger than themselves. They did not take an easy route. They did not have that option.

<u>Number two,</u> I wanted to pass along some of the history I had heard throughout my life. The Wood family is a good bunch of people. They did not even start out as farmers, but they adjusted and made the most of it.

<u>The third reason</u> is I wanted to pass these stories along to the generations who will follow. Hopefully, children, grandchildren, great grandchildren, etc. will feel like a part of a bigger story.

<u>Number four</u> I wanted to share the faith of my parents. They moved away from the family they loved for five years to print gospel tracts for missionaries around the world. The faith that changed their lives, is the same faith I want to share with readers who have eyes to see and ears to hear.

<u>Finally,</u> I wanted to see if I could rise to the challenge of writing a book. I must say it has been one of the more enjoyable projects I have taken on in my life.

Introduction

Allow me to introduce myself. My name is Keith Wood. I was born on March 4, 1946 and raised by a young couple, who would later farm in Southwest Iowa. I am pretty sure as they brought me home from the hospital, they were in way over their heads. They had both sets of parents upset with them within their first four years of marriage.

I have been in over my head often in my life as well, so I have forgiven them for their parenting shortfalls. I have done a lot of different things in my life. None of them are all that earth shaking, but I would like to share them with you if you have the time to sit with me. I will do my best to make them interesting for you.

For those of you who have already read more than you care to, I have the Cliffs notes version; and believe me I know about Cliffs notes. Here are my life's highlights and major changes.

Leaving the farm
Going to college at UNI
Becoming a teacher at North Scott School District
Being drafted into the Army and going to Viet Nam
Falling in love with Doris and her Jesus
Falling in love with learning
Desiring to write it down

As I write about my life in short stories, I will share what life was like during the good and bad times. I have lived much of my life planning for what's next, asking if there is a better way, and asking myself why did I make that decision?

For example, I skipped freshman orientation the day after I arrived at college. What could I possibly have had to do that would have been more important to my well being? Did my socks need folding? Was I behind in rolling up my toothpaste tube? God only knows, but there I was in my fourth story dorm room confident that I would be able to breeze through the University of Northern Iowa. After all I was a member of the National Honor Society. I was ranked sixth in my high school graduating class of 40.

Within three months, I was in a UNI counselor's office trying to figure out why 10 of my 16 hours had a 'D' grade next to them. I did not enjoy reading, and every class I was taking had a textbook the size of a Quad-City phone book. I truly was in over my head.

Arthur and Femmie's Family

Front Row (left to right)   Arthur, Arden, and Femmie Wood
Middle Row (left to right) Lucille, Mildred, and Doris Wood
Back Row (left to right)   Bruce, Ralph, and Clyde Wood

Wood Family Line in this book

Arthur Stephen Wood & Femmie Estella Chapman
born Sep 13, 1881   born Feb 10, 1889
(married June 15, 1910)

Their Children

Clyde	Mildred	Ralph	Bruce	Lucille	Doris	**Arden**
Jul 1912	Feb 1914	Oct 1915	Oct 1917	Dec 1919	Jul 1921	Nov 1924
(Phyllis)	(Burnell Byer)	(Maxine)	(Clara)	(Ralph Neal)	(Lloyd Chaloupka)	(Norma Jean)

Arden and Norma Jean's Five Boys

Keith Duane	Carroll Dean	Larry Lee	Dean Arthur	Marvin Rex
Mar 1946	Sep 1947	Dec 1949	Jan 1952	Aug 1954
(Doris Jess)	(Linda Raasch)	(Judy Shannon)	(Charlene Bass)	(Mary Vasbinder)

Wood Family Line

Chapter 1

The Great Depression

It was late fall in the year 1933. Arthur Wood was one frustrated, upset, 52-year-old Iowa farmer. He had been talking to an official at the Orient Bank. The bank representative was reminding him once again that if he did not keep up on his loan payments they had no choice but to foreclose on their family farm. Arthur did not doubt the man's word. He had seen other neighbors go out of business and sell their farms. Arthur and his wife, Femmie, had planned to live out their lives farming this farm. In better times, the farm had provided well for them.

Femmie did not say much when her husband was this upset. She trusted him. He really was quite sharp when it came to financial matters. Arthur took care of all their business dealings. He always shared with her any problems they were facing. The farm economy just would not give them a break. It had taken a turn for the worse for four years now. Working harder just could not compete with low farm prices year after year.

Likewise, their seven children were avoiding talking to their father. They knew how upset he could get when they did something wrong. But this was a problem no one in the Wood household could correct. They would have gladly offered a remedy if they had had a clue on how to solve their dad's financial problems.

The two older boys, Clyde (21) and Ralph (18), had graduated from Orient High School and were committed to farming with their father. Like so many at that time, they followed the occupation of their father. Mildred (19), the daughter between them in age, was going to Iowa State Teachers College (now UNI) to become a teacher. Financial support for her was certainly limited. She was working her way through college.

Bruce (16) was completing his junior year at Orient High School. He drove the school bus before and after school, just as his older brothers had done. The Wood family had a contract with the school district to drive the bus. If the boys were too busy for any reason, Arthur himself, had to drive the bus.

Lucille (14) and Doris (13) were attending their respective classes at Orient. A seventh child, Harold, had died 3 months after his birth. And finally, my father, Arden, who was soon to be 10 years old. He was watching and learning as all this drama unfolded.

Every one of these children knew Arthur was under a lot of stress. There was not as much laughter around the table, as in earlier times. They were all learning the consequences of what can happen when the farm economy goes bad. They were all to soon learn about foreclosure.

The Great Depression began in 1929 as a recession. The Stock Market crashed in October 1929. Within the next five years, 15 million Americans (more than 20% of the population) were unemployed. More than half of the country's banks had failed. Over one million farm families lost their farms between 1930 and 1934.

President Herbert Hoover, widely blamed for not doing enough, lost the election of 1932 to Franklin Delano Roosevelt in a landslide. FDR's plan called the 'New Deal', brought on unprecedented programs for relief, recovery, and reform.

There were programs that paid farmers to take farmland out of production. Another program put unemployed workers to work for the Civilian Conservation Corps (CCC). Dad called them the 'CC' boys. This was a public work relief program that operated from 1933 to 1942 for unemployed, unmarried men.

The men of the CCC worked on construction projects throughout the country. They planted over three billion trees. They improved over 800 national parks. Dad told me some of his immediate family took advantage of this program. It is one of those family things I wish I had delved into more. Since he was younger at the time, he did not know which of his family had worked as 'CC' boys.

Men enlisted for a minimum of six months. Dad said a farmer with a team of horses and a scraper could make five times as much as the common laborer. It is estimated nearly three million men, about 5% of the total U.S population, took part in this program. Men were provided with shelter, clothing, and food with a wage of $30 per month (about $570 per month in 2017 dollars). They were required to send $22 to $25 of their pay back home.

Another program for farmers allowed farmers to seal (store) corn in a corn crib for 45 cents a bushel. This was one way farmers were able to get some much needed cash. It also helped if a family had to move, since they did not have to move all that corn in a short amount of time.

Arthur had corn piled everywhere, according to Dad. Every ear was picked by hand and thrown into a horse-drawn, steel-wheeled wagon. Think of all the work involved in picking that corn, shoveling it into piles around the farm, and re-shoveling it into wagons to take to Orient.

One of the problems of the time was that farmers had produced too much corn. That surplus had driven corn prices down to eight to ten cents a bushel. Some farmers started burning corn for fuel rather than buying coal because corn was so cheap.

To get much needed cash, farmers flooded the market with livestock. This action resulted in livestock prices going way down. Many farmers could not make their mortgage payments. Farms were foreclosed on by the banks, who had loaned money to buy farms and to provide operating cash for the year.

In many ways, the farmers were better off than city folks as they could grow large gardens. They butchered their own cattle and chickens for meat. They could hunt for game if the meat supply got low. There was a lot of rabbit and squirrel eaten during the depression years. With minimal jobs and money, farmers could at least put food on the table. They did not have to experience the soup lines found in cities.

People bartered with each other for needed items and services due to the shortage of cash. One mother might trade some of her garden produce to a neighbor who raised chickens. An electrician might be hired in exchange for a big load of fire wood. A half of beef or a pig would be tempting to those with something to trade.

There was a lot of anger and frustration as neighbor after neighbor was forced to sell everything and move on. Farmers were not allowed to purchase back the farm they had just lost. Arthur was one of those angry men. He swore, "If I ever get out of this mess they will never put my back to the wall again."

Arthur did receive a major break. He was paid $3,000 for all the corn he sealed at the Orient elevator. It just so happened he owed his father-in-law, John Chapman, $3,000. John was 76 years old at the time. Considering the financial distress of the nation, and more specifically the distress of his oldest daughter's family, John told Arthur and Femmie to keep the $3,000 as part of their inheritance.

John told them they could purchase a good 80-acre farm and not be too much in debt, or they could purchase a larger farm, which would provide a home and employment for the whole family. Since jobs were practically non-existent for everyone, Arthur decided on a 320-acre farm between Yale and Panora, Iowa.

Arthur was not one to show his emotions, but he was deeply moved by the generosity of his father-in-law. In 1934, $3,000 was a great deal of money. Arthur knew he had to do something, and now he had the resources to do it.

Chapter 2

The Wood Family Moves

It was the early spring of 1934. It had turned cold, and yet, it was time to move on to the 320-acre farm near Yale and Panora, from the Orient farmstead that had served them well for 15 years. Arthur had been one of the more established farmers in the area. He had a herd of purebred Angus beef cattle. Their house was as modern as any in the area. They were one of the first to have an indoor toilet. They owned a car, a 1927 Whippet coach. And yet, they could not make it through the depression.

There were lots of memories, some good and some not so good, in this house; lots of dreams, lots of meals, lots of cards, lots of family camaraderie. Lucille, Doris, and Arden had been born in this house. One son, Harold, died shortly after his birth. They had to leave his grave behind, in the northeast corner of the Orient Cemetery.

They were moving away from a good neighbor, Henry Hainline, and his family. They were the owners of the fox farm, known for raising foxes for their pelts. In fact, Doris was going to stay with this family until the school year was over. Henry's fox farm had special memories for Arden. The owner charged people 10 cents to see all the animals they were raising for their furs. It was like going to the zoo for Arden. He often got to visit for free.

If you were to look up these properties today, you need to go two miles south of Orient on Highway 25. Then go one mile east on 330th St. to Quebec Ave. and turn right. The first property on the right is the old Wood family farm (mailing address, 3310 Quebec Ave., Creston, Iowa). Just a little further south on the opposite side of the rode is the former Hainline fox farm.

Arthur and Femmie had signed the proper ownership papers to transfer the two farms. It would have been nice to wait for warmer weather, but that was not an option. Hesitantly, the three family members bundled up in the early morning, Arthur (Grandpa Wood), and his two oldest sons, Clyde and Ralph, ages 21 and 18. They were joined by two other men - Verne Wallace, a cousin, and Joe Pickerell, a family friend.

Three teams of horses were pulling wagons loaded with grain and various farm implements. Two men were riding horses. Their job was to corral the ten Angus beef cattle walking alongside. Tied onto the back of each wagon were more horses. It was the cheapest way to get all this property moved. It made for a long single file caravan of horse teams. The drivers got off every so often to walk alongside this slow moving procession. It was a means of keeping warm.

The men headed north two miles on Quebec Ave., then two miles east on East Division St, (G61), and seven miles north on Henry Wallace Rd/Sheldon Ave. If you get out your trusty Iowa map, or Google maps for those who are tech savvy, you can see the route they took. Next they went three miles east on Highway 92, and 14 miles north on the Stuart Road (P28) to Stuart.

With a little quick calculation, you realize they went 28 miles in one day. That left a 20 mile trip for the second day. The second day they traveled north on Wagon Road (P38) and Iowa Highway 4. Can you imagine going 48 miles in cold weather at the speed of big Belgian horses plodding along? There was no way to speed up if you expected the horses to pull this load all day.

Grandpa Wood had a pre-arranged plan to stay on a friend's farm near Stuart overnight. Supposedly the farm they stayed at was near the current McDonald's in Stuart. The men and their horses needed to be rested and fed, if they were to survive on this two-day trip. For the young and daring - I would challenge you to try biking this route. Let me know and I will join you, Lord willing. Much of the route is now paved, but there are a lot of hills.

Bruce, Lucille, Doris and Arden were not part of this long cold trip as they were still in school. Bruce and Doris were staying behind with other families in the Orient area to complete their school year. Lucille was moving to enroll in the high school at Yale. My father, Arden, was 10, the youngest of this bunch. He would enroll in a Guthrie County country school, as soon as his mother, Lucille, and he could get moved to the new 320-acre farm.

One interesting sidelight was the fact that these men talked to people along the way as they traveled. Years later, they realized that Ralph had talked with his future father-in-law while walking along the stretch of road north of Panora.

The new farm was on Highway 17 (later changed to Highway 4) two miles north of the Brethren Church. Coming in from the north, it is located a half- mile west of Yale, and one and a half miles south on the west side of the road.

The farm had a large house which had been used as a stagecoach depot in earlier years. It also had two big barns and a corn crib south of the house that was 96 feet long. According to Dad, it took a lot of man hours to fill the corn crib when picking corn by hand.

As time passed, Grandpa Wood tried to help each of his children get established on their own farms. He did that without ever putting an additional mortgage on the original 320 acres. Years later, Grandpa wanted to buy 40 more acres east of the house. His wife, Femmie, Clyde and Ralph were against it. One of them said, "Haven't you had enough?" He accepted their judgment.

Grandpa, Clyde and Ralph farmed together using shared machinery. Clyde and Ralph even had a shared car for quite a while. Dad mentioned that Clyde was scared to step out on his own, after what his Dad had been through in the depression. Clyde bought a "B" John Deere tractor and a plow for $800; he could not sleep at night because of the debt. The depression had a lasting impression on the whole family.

Grandpa Wood bought his first tractor some years after 1935. He spent most of his farming life working with horses. He really liked and took care of his horses. He got after any of the boys if they abused his prized animals. Grandpa bought horses whenever he saw one priced right. He trained them to work as teams and finally sold them if he had more than enough of his own. In fact, Dad said people came from all around to buy horses from Grandpa.

Grandpa never did feel comfortable driving a tractor. Dad said Grandpa herded the tractor rather than driving it. I am not quite sure what that means. Grandpa never had more than a 5th grade education. My mother was always impressed with the way he could figure things out in his head while others were finding a pencil and paper to do the calculations.

When I asked Dad how his sisters fit into the work plan, he thought awhile. He finally responded saying, "The ladies worked inside and the men worked outside." Dad also said six of the seven children raised by Arthur and Femmie, found their marriage partners within six miles of the family farm. Mildred was the one exception.

All but Bruce made a living farming, at least for a while. Bruce went to college in Indiana. The only times he came back to the farm were to visit. Dad hardly ever spoke of Bruce, even though Bruce was successful in all his education and ministry endeavors. Bruce and Clara spent four years in Poland after World War II, working on the reconstruction. Both went on to teach and minister in Montana and California.

In his younger years, Dad always considered college a waste of money and time. He had never done real well in school himself. Bruce's success in school, and Dad's struggles were no doubt related to Dad's lack of enthusiasm when I spoke of going to college.

The economy changed after those depression years. Grandpa and Grandma did quite well financially on the 320 acres. The land was much better land than the land he had near Orient.

My brother Carroll said Grandpa bought another 400 acres near Springbrook State Park. Dale Neal said Grandpa bought a field on the edge of Panora that his dad, Ralph Neal, farmed until he retired from farming. Grandpa, like many in our family, was not one to sit around in retirement. He bought a furniture store in Panora, working with his son-in-law, Bunny Byer. These two also had a Skelgas franchise selling propane bottled gas.

After Grandpa and Grandma passed away, Dad and Mom inherited enough money to make a good payment on their farm and build a new, much needed farm house. In the Wood tradition, every heir got the same amount. Every one of Grandpa and Grandma's 26 grandchildren inherited $1,000 toward a college education, or their chosen professions. I know I was impressed. That was a good sum of money for a poor college student.

Financially Grandpa Wood had done quite well. He bought and sold as long as he could, until his memory failed him, and he had to live out the final part of his life in the Guthrie Center Nursing Home.

Team of horses hitched to a wagon full of corn

Arthur Wood's car getting washed

Single Row Cultivator

From left to right - Great-grandpa John Chapman, Grandpa Arthur Wood, Ralph Wood, Arden Wood (front), and Bruce Wood

Chapter 3

Mom Grew Up in Poverty

My Mother, Norma Jean, was the oldest of five children. Hershel and Hazel were extremely poor. Mom described her early, temporary home as a one room, 8' by 15' cabin that could be pulled around on skids. I have four bedrooms bigger than that. Her privacy was the great outdoors.

She described her father, Hershel, as a day laborer. He worked as a hired man most of his life. He would work 10 hours a day to earn one dollar. Mom's family moved often to wherever Hershel could find work. Mom wrote on the subject, "I can remember nine different homes that we had. Most of them were trailer houses provided for the hired man."

When Hershel was out of work they moved their little cabin close to her mother's parents, Claude and Flora Tallman. Mom wrote, "Grandpa and Grandma Tallman were always available to us. We often had Sunday dinner with them."

Mom gave her life to Jesus at age 12 in a small church in Wichita, Iowa, at a revival meeting. Going to church was a big part of her social life. In fact she met Dad at a youth function at the church.

She was committed to getting a high school education. She stayed with her grandmother at times during the winter so she could get to Guthrie Center High School. The back roads they lived on were often impassible in the winter. Getting an education meant a lot to Mom.

Her first full-time job was teaching at a country school. She did that for two years. I'm sure she did quite well, just because she cared for young people so much. However, Mom said she never really felt comfortable as a teacher. Her short stature, of just over five feet meant that some of her older students were taller and stronger than she was.

As I mentioned earlier, Dad and Mom met at a church social. They were both attracted to each other right from the start. To hear Dad tell it there were several girls interested in him. Unfortunately, I never got Mom's insight on this, but she was never one to disagree with Dad. She would just laugh and let him go on talking. It does seem amazing that these two people from rather different backgrounds found their way together.

Dad was a young farmer working with his father. At some point, quite a bit later, Dad decided that Mom was more special than any of the other girls. Mom was ready for a committed life as soon as Dad was willing to humble himself and admit he wanted her too.

The delay was longer than you might have thought, however, because Mom was engaged to another man who went into the service. After several nervous discussions, and Mom calling off her engagement, Mom and Dad committed themselves to each other.

The strange conclusion of this courtship is that Mom's father, Hershel, did not approve of their marriage. In fact he did not even attend their wedding in spite of some rather pointed words from his own family. One comment from his mother-in-law was something like, "Hershel, you will regret skipping this wedding for the rest of your life."

From what I know of the people expressing these sentiments, the words would have been much stronger than the words I used. His wife, Hazel, and his mother-in-law, Flora, had no problem finding expressive names and direct words when they were upset.

Arden and Norma Jean were married anyway. They lived with Grandpa and Grandma Wood for four years, farming Grandpa's 320-acre farm. During those years the first two sons, myself and Carroll were born. A trip to Des Moines was deemed necessary for both births.

When I was four years old, Dad and Mom decided they needed to move. I can only imagine there had to be lots of discussion and a few raised voices as Dad decided he wanted to farm on his own. Mom's character was such that she would have supported Dad in whatever he chose. Grandpa Wood's character was strong enough, however, that they both would have known that he was not pleased with their decision. Dad was determined to try it on his own.

Chapter 4

Getting to Know Mom Better

Mom had her faults and she would have been the first person to admit that. However, I have heard her nominated for sainthood more times than any other person I know. Those doing the nominating included daughters-in-law, sons and fellow church members. Others have said Mom had six boys to raise.

Mom was a quiet, unassuming person who was intensely loyal to her husband, her boys, her family, her church, and her neighborhood. People were always welcome in her house. From a family standpoint, it has been said, "Dad was out there bringing people in, but it was Mom who made them not want to leave."

In those days wives were expected to be subject to their husbands. Mom was obedient to a fault. As a son watching the family dynamic, I wondered why Mom did not speak up more. She worked from sun up to sun down. She worked in the house and outside the house. She was expected to come when Dad needed something. Whatever he was doing was more important than what she was doing.

She washed clothes each Monday with a wringer washer and hung them out to dry. She baked bread, which always included those great smelling cinnamon rolls. She killed, dressed, butchered, and cooked chickens at least once a week.

After Dad plowed the garden, the rest was up to Mom. She was in charge of all shopping. She did all the cooking and dishwashing because after all, that was women's work.

We would come home from church on some Sundays and find a car load of relatives waiting to be welcomed in and fed. Dad grumbled under his breath, but Mom had a smile on her face as she welcomed these guests in.

Through the hard times, Mom always knew how to add more water to the soup. I grew up not liking soup as it was always so watery. We used a lot of saltine crackers just adding substance to the soup. Dad and the five boys really wanted meat, potatoes and gravy at every meal.

Most every night the family had a card game. Mom thoroughly enjoyed playing cards with this rowdy bunch, but she never joined in until all the dishes were done and she had popped a huge bowl of popcorn.

Mom was the counselor when one of the five boys couldn't meet Dad's standards. She stopped and talked to us, even though she herself was subject to Dad's controlling ways.

Mom was the encourager and the letter writer. To this day I am embarrassed at how rarely I wrote her. Still, she faithfully wrote. She would give me a bunch of postcards so I could drop her a line from college. They would still be there at the end of the semester. I am sure I got a letter from her every week while I was in Viet Nam, maybe two.

During my last month in Viet Nam I made plans to visit my Army buddy in the Los Angeles area. When the time finally arrived to fly back to the states, there was no way I was stopping anywhere. I wanted to see Mom, and the family.

God bless you Mom. I miss you.

Chapter 5

Getting to Know Dad Better

I have found Dad hard to write about. I have spent a disproportionate amount of time in my life trying to understand him. Mom was so easy to write about. She was humble. She was willing to listen. She cared about what was important to you.

Dad, not so much. He and I had trouble just having a two-way discussion. I saw him as being controlling. With age, he repeated stories over and over. I would guess there are at least 100 stories that my four brothers and I could easily finish.

As he aged and I matured, I found myself being more sympathetic to him and actually loving him. Dad had no ill will in all his talking. He just could not allow there to be silence. I can't even count the number of times Dad said to me, "Well I am doing all the talking. What is happening with you?" He would always catch me off guard with that statement. While I was pondering what Dad would be interested in hearing, he would start talking again, and that was the end of what was happening in my life.

I can not begin to imagine how many times Mom must have heard Dad tell the same stories over and over. Mom liked to read. She could tune him out, along with his football or baseball game on TV. But there was never any question that talking trumped reading.

Dad did not enjoy reading. According to him he never learned to read well. He was a slow reader. During the second half of his life, each morning he read the Bible and the current copy of Our Daily Bread. He shared with me during his last year that he had read the Bible through six times.

Dad liked to talk to people. He did not allow people to be strangers for long. On Sunday mornings, he roamed the church poking, talking and teasing people. Dad loved to tease people, especially attractive young ladies. But this teasing and harassing was not limited to the church.

The nurses in health facilities and nursing homes knew who Dad was. He never wanted the door to his room closed. He wanted to see and tease the nurses as they passed by. He had been told and truly believed that he had a gift for cheering people up. And he did cheer people up. Once he knew you, and liked you, you were fair game.

Dad was the youngest of seven, born to Arthur and Femme Wood. Since his dad Arthur was a farmer, I don't think my dad even considered any other occupation. One thing I am certain about is both he and his dad knew how to work hard and expected others to be just as diligent.

Dad and I never saw eye to eye while I was living on the home farm. I was a shy, thoughtful person with pretty low self-esteem. Dad did not have a real high regard for education. He made it clear that he thought going to college was a waste of time and money. I probably would have given in to his logic if I had known how to make a respectable living without going to college. The one thing I did know was, I was not going to farm with Dad.

For many reasons, Dad was always concerned about finances. I doubt there was ever a time when Dad felt like he was fiscally secure. He was concerned about making a living for his family. He told each of us boys that upon graduation from high school we were moving out or paying rent. It wasn't that he didn't love us or want the best for us. It was that we were adults at that point, and we had to pull our own weight.

Dad was a buyer and seller. He would buy things at farm sales or garage sales that he thought he could refurbish and then sell for a profit. He had an older brother, Clyde, who offered to supply him cash to do more buying and selling. Dad turned him down. He was afraid he might lose money. Clyde offered to help Dad and Mom buy more land. They turned him down again for fear they might end up losing the farm they had worked so hard to own. The last depression had taught Mom and Dad well.

The year after I left for college, in 1965, Dad tore down the drafty, old farm home and constructed a new one on the same spot, while still farming. Obviously he had some carpentry skills.

I was told Dad had some sort of nervous breakdown between 1973 and 1975. His doctor advised him to sell the farm and do something else. The farm was sold in the spring of 1975. Mom and Dad moved to Creston, where Dad became a full time carpenter, working for himself. The community college wanted Dad to take on some interns. Dad wisely turned them down. He was not a patient teacher. Dad never saw mistakes as learning opportunities. To him, mistakes were to be pointed out and corrected, probably by him.

That change in occupation must have boded well for Dad's health. In 1981 he and a brother-in-law, Ralph Neal, bought four lots in Panora. Panora was Mom and Dad's old stomping grounds. Most of the Wood family still lived there. Ralph and Dad then proceeded to build a house for each of their empty nest families. The plan was to build a third house and sell it. Dad and Ralph's relationship was a huge success as they both were Christian men who respected each other.

With two houses built, Dad felt the Lord was leading him and Mom to move to Indiana to work for World Missionary Press. I knew he and Mom were growing in their relationship with the Lord, but I did not realize how much. All of Dad's brothers tried to discourage him from making such an extreme change in career. However, when Dad made up his mind, he was not easily persuaded otherwise.

In the summer of 1986 Dad and Mom pulled up stakes and moved to New Paris, Indiana. They were volunteers, printing gospel tracts, and scripture booklets, in many languages, to be used by missionaries throughout the world. Dad was a press operator and supervisor of volunteers. They made a lot of close friends during that time. After five years, and mom's serious illness, they decided it was time for them to move back to Iowa and be around all the family they had left behind.

Moving back to Des Moines they became examples of hospitality. Their house was a warm and friendly meeting place for any who would stop by to visit. Mom would be offering a glass of lemonade or soda pop, and any baked treat she had available. Probably within 15 minutes, cards were being shuffled if the guests were up for cards. Mom's cousin, Vera, and her husband, Larry, were frequent visitors and card players. The women loved beating the men. The competition was intense with lots of good-natured ribbing, both during and after the game.

In their later years, Mom and Dad helped each other get around well enough they could stay in their own home with little or no assistance. They celebrated their 70th wedding anniversary on February 11, 2015 about a month before Mom died. One of her last wishes was to live to celebrate this special anniversary. It pleased her greatly to have made it, and to greet all their old friends and relatives. Dad was in a nursing home shortly thereafter. He never quite recovered from losing Mom. He died two years later at the age of 92. He was a good Christian man.

I was able to get closer to Dad in his last 10 years of life. He trusted me, and all his sons, to do the best things for him. I was his power of attorney and my brother, Marvin, was their health care power of attorney. Marvin and his wife Mary lived ten miles away from the folks. Marvin and I got to spend lots of time together, deciding what the next move should be, as the folks health deteriorated. It was tough watching Dad go down hill. He had been such a strong person for so many years.

I think it really hurt Dad in his last two years of life to realize that he had outlived his money. Their knee surgeries and hip replacements, their ambulance calls and hospital stays, their time in hospice used money faster than low interest CD's could produce it.

Mom and Dad had always planned that their house would be their estate to hand on to the boys. Now, even that was spoken for by the government that had provided so many services.

Dad said he was relieved for Mom, that she did not know how poor they were. I really think Mom would have taken it in stride. Being broke really bothered Dad, as I guess it would have bothered anyone who had worked so hard all their life to own a farm, feed his family, and not be a burden to any of those he loved.

Several people, including myself, had to talk long and hard to get Dad to accept the fact that other church members wanted to take him to church. He was a proud man when it came to accepting help.

His church treated him like a king and he soaked it up. I would watch him at church greeting and poking everyone who came by. It was like a ritual for many of the members to pass by and joke with Dad.

As his health went down hill, he needed more help. I cherished the time we had together in those last months. I think he and I really respected each other in his last days on earth. When he passed, I felt the whole family was happy for him. He was finally back with Mom, and now, with Jesus.

Chapter 6

History According to Dad

Dad was the youngest of the Arthur Wood family and the last of the immediate family to pass away. It bothered him that what he knew about his immediate family would be lost when he died. United States history or world history were subjects he would have had to read about in school. The fact that he did not enjoy reading or studying history guarantees he knew little on these subjects. I never heard him talk much about WWII. America's involvement in the war happened when he was 17-21 years old. It may have been embarrassing that he did not serve when friends around him did.

Obviously all of Arthur and Femmie's sons and son-in-laws could have enlisted for military service. They were all of service age. Many boys their age had already signed up to join the war effort. This has been called "The Greatest Generation." The country was united in its commitment to stop Germany and Japan, who were attempting to take control of the world.

No doubt the subject of the war came up around the dinner table or their Sunday afternoon discussions. There is a very good chance some of their friends and classmates were already training for war or had been shipped out. The thing these boys had going for them was their '2C' farm labor classification.

Farm laborers were considered crucial to the war effort, and were thus encouraged to stay on the farm.

It is impossible to know how much the Wood family knew of what was happening with the war, with Hitler and the Holocaust. It is fair to say that they were probably more concerned about the farm economy than they were about what was happening in Europe and the Pacific.

Consequently, history to Dad was passing on his life experiences to the next generation. So the bulk of Chapter 6 contains stories that Dad would have shared with anyone who would listen.

The history Dad passed along was built around four generations of the Wood family. That line went from Arthur Wood, to Joseph Wood, to Arthur Stephen Wood (my grandfather), to Arden Royce Wood (my father).

The first Arthur Wood was born in England in 1817. He married Margaret Jackson Wood in Blackburn, England in 1842. Arthur was a weaver and made his living by that trade. Their three oldest children, two boys and a baby girl, were born in England. The oldest son's name was Joseph, the next in our line of ancestors. In 1848, the Wood family boarded a ship and moved to the United States. It took them six weeks to make that ocean journey. The family settled in the state of Rhode Island, where Arthur worked as a weaver in the cotton mills. In those days, some children worked long days along with their parents, earning money for the family. There is a good chance that Joseph and his younger brother, James, went to work in the mills. Arthur and Margaret had three more children in the United States.

Some men convinced Arthur he should come to Iowa. Supposedly, big ships could come up the Shanghai River and dock in Nevinville, Iowa. It seems there was a promotion to get people to move to Nevinville. Arthur bought some land with the idea of starting a mill of some kind, to take advantage of this situation. He moved west with two of his daughters. When he got to his land he found out the Shanghai River was only a big ditch and Nevinville was only a stop in the road with a couple of stores and two churches.

Arthur and the two girls nearly starved that first winter. They knew nothing about farming. In time they learned. They planted a grove. They built a somewhat comfortable home. The whole family moved to Iowa in 1868 and became a farm family. According to the notes I have, there are still remnants of the grove, building foundations, and a cement cellar if you find the right place on the southwest corner of the original 160 acres. I can not verify that. Arthur died in 1895. Margaret passed away in 1885. They are buried in the Orient cemetery.

Maggie Burbanks, who lived north of Creston, confirmed the story of the original Arthur Wood family almost starving, as her mother was the youngest of Arthur Wood's daughters. She said they would see squirrels in the trees, but they had no way to kill them for food. Arthur Stephen Wood (my grandfather) and Maggie Burbanks were first cousins.

Joseph Wood, Arthur and Margaret's oldest son, was born in England in 1843. He married Mary Jane (Jennie) Smart Wood in 1858. They had five children including, Arthur Stephen (my grandfather), Esther (Edsall), Cora (Wallace), Jim, and George.

Joseph continued in the farm life buying a 160-acre farm near his father's land. Joseph and Mary Jane Wood are buried in the Pleasant Grove cemetery.

In 1919, Arthur (Joseph and Mary Jane's oldest son) and Femmie Chapman Wood moved their young family to their Orient farm. They planned to live there for the rest of their lives. That was before the Depression. For more information on this farm, go back to Chapters 1 and 2 of this book. There was a Pleasant Grove Church and cemetery in the area. Several of the Chapmans owned farm land just north of the church.

Femmie's grandparents, Milton and Elizabeth Chapman helped organize the Pleasant Grove Church (four miles south of Fontanelle) and were charter members. They are buried in the Pleasant Grove Cemetery. The Pleasant Grove Church has been torn down, but several of our early family members are buried in the cemetery, including Arthur and Femmies' parents. Their names are Joseph and Mary Jane Wood and John and Melissa Chapman. Someone has updated their grave stones so they are easy to read.

Dad told this story every time someone at our meal table did not like the food that was being served. It seems the Arthur Wood family was gathered for the evening meal. Young Arden made the comment that some part of his mother's meal did not taste good. Everyone's eyes at the table turned to him. Then everyone's eyes shifted to his dad. Arthur did not disappoint. He told young Arden he must not be all that hungry and that he was excused from the table. The next morning he did not complain about breakfast. He was ready to eat.

Dad liked to tell the fox farm story. Henry Hainline had a fox farm close by the Wood farm. Arthur rented Henry's farm land to raise a field of oats. On this particular day the men were shocking oats in sweltering heat. Arthur and the older boys had sent Arden to the house to get a gallon jug of cold water. As Arden went by the fox farm he met Henry with a big load of ground meat. It was time to feed all the animals.

Henry asked Arden if he would like to go along and watch. Arden answered, "I don't have a dime." Henry smiled and said he would not charge him. What an opportunity! Arden jumped on the meat wagon. He had the time of his life until he had to face the thirsty oat shockers. The only thing that saved him from severe discipline was Henry taking the blame for calling him away.

From Orient, the Arthur Wood family moved to the Panora and Yale area. This was a 320-acre farm with a very large farm home. My parents and grandparents shared the house when my folks were first married in 1945. We lived in the west side of the house. The house was big enough for both of our families. As preschoolers, Carroll and I had no qualms about going over to see our grandparents. Dad always said our mother and grandmother got along really well together`.

Dad told the story about the 96-foot-long corn crib on the homestead leaning, and getting worse. They were feeling bad that they were going to have to tear it down. One night a big storm came through the area. When they went out the next morning, they noted that the corn crib was standing straight up again. The men rushed around putting braces on every side of the building. The reinforced corn crib served them for many more years.

There was a unique water source half a mile northwest of the house. Dad always called it the 'Ram'. It was kind of a piston device that forced water to the house and the surrounding area. Dad showed some of us boys the 'Ram' at work. It was drawing water from an underground spring, according to him. The whole system looked very wasteful as over half the water spilled out on the ground. There was a wooden cover over it to keep any foreign objects out.

When it worked properly, it was great, according to Dad. And it did work properly most of the time. The water was cold and tasted good. Then one year it did not work well. They purchased a new 'Ram'. They even had a 'Ram' specialist come out to get it to work properly. Neither this expert, nor others who tried later, could get it to work as it should. They finally offered $100 to anyone who could make it work.

A local blacksmith out of Yale came out armed with a wooden shingle and a small hammer. He just kept tapping until the system was perfectly level. When it was in just the right position, the new 'Ram' started working. What a relief to have running water again.

Unfortunately, a big discussion ensued as to whether this blacksmith had done enough to be worth $100. Alas, he was given $25 for his efforts. Both sides of the argument went away grumbling, even though they were both better off. The 'Ram' was working again, and the blacksmith would have had to work quite a while to earn $25 blacksmithing.

A couple of home restorers purchased this grand old house, trying to make it become what it once had been. They moved it just north of Happy Acres Lake (Diamondhead Lake) near Stuart, Iowa where it stands today.

The Better Homes and Gardens channel made a TV show of the moving of the house. Dad and Mom made a trip from Des Moines to watch the old house being moved. I saw it on TV the first time they showed it. I have never seen it shown again. I thought at the time, Better Homes and Gardens really missed an opportunity by not interviewing Aunt Doris and Dad, who had lived in the house.

Dad tells about the Armistice Day storm, that happened on November 11, 1940. Guthrie Center and Panora were to play their last football game of the season. Since it was a holiday they were expecting a big crowd.

The storm that ensued was later called the storm of the century. Temperatures plummeted from 60 degrees to below freezing, and then into single digits—all within a matter of hours. Raging winds delivered pelting rain which quickly turned to sleet, then heavy snow.

By the time the storm had stopped, it had dropped more than two feet of snow, buried vehicles and roadways beneath 20-foot drifts, killed thousands of Iowa cattle, and destroyed incalculable amounts of poultry—including more than a million Thanksgiving turkeys. All told, the storm claimed 160 human lives. Many duck hunters lost their lives during this storm, dressed in light clothing because the day had started so warm.

Needless to say, the game was postponed. Since Panora wouldn't let their school buses go out, Panora residents opened their homes to the rural students. Dad remembers being stuck in Panora, and that his Dad was upset because he wasn't home to do chores.

To finish these random stories from Dad, I will pass along a quote from Grandpa Wood, "Everyone should be drug through the mud at least once, preferably face down, and when he gets up he would gladly talk to anyone, rich or poor."

The vast majority of Dad's immediate family are buried in the eastern section of the Church of the Brethren cemetery approximately two miles north of Panora. The Brethren Church is the church that most of the Wood family attended over the years while they farmed. Mom and Dad are buried there, within 20 yards of his parents. Doris and Lloyd Chaloupka's graves are the farthest away. You can find their graves by heading south on the path going through the center of the cemetery.

Dad's brother Ralph Wood, and his wife, Maxine, donated their bodies to the University of Iowa for the medical school to study. Their bodies were cremated and their remains scattered on their family farm.

If you go north from the church on Highway 4 for a couple miles, you will go past the area of the original family farm on the left. Doris's daughter, Gladys Chaloupka Willey, currently lives there with her husband, Norman Willey. Stop in and say hi if you are in the area. You can thank me later, Gladys.

Trying to be a good investigative reporter, I emailed Gladys and Norman to get a status on the corn crib, the 'Ram', and the stately old house. This would be a follow up on the stories Dad had told over the years.

Norman wrote me a short book on the problems he and Lloyd Chaloupka, his father-in-law, have had over the years. The corn crib has been torn down after years of continually adding more supports. The 'Ram' no longer works and has been a nightmare of erosion, wet land, and snakes. It seems that the water source is much bigger than a spring and much harder to control.

Norman pointed out the old house was older than the town of Yale. The house was built in 1879 and Yale's centennial was in 1982. Over the years, the house has been a continual maintenance problem. They have fixed the foundation, the roof, windows, ceilings, plaster, etc.

Since all of these problems go beyond the scope of this book, I will let you talk to Norman if you want to know more. Thank you, Norman, for the information.

As an add on, in May of 2018, the four children of Doris and Lloyd Chaloupka, Joyce, Jean, Duane, and Gladys, along with my wife, Doris, and I drove the route that Arthur and his family traveled during the Depression. To say the least, we were impressed with the efforts of our forefathers to move the 48 miles from Orient to Panora in the middle of winter. My brother, Larry, and wife, Judy, joined us to guide us around the Orient area.

On the way back, we stopped to see the stately old house being restored north of Diamondhead Lake. The exterior looks very attractive surrounded by a well manicured lawn. What a project this couple has taken on. I was overwhelmed by all the work they had done to this old house, and the immense amount of work that still lays ahead of them. This couple has to be close to 70 years old. What a couple of troopers.

Arthur and Femmies 50th Wedding Anniversary

Front row (left to right) - Bunny and Mildred Byer, Arthur and Femmie Wood, Norma Jean and Arden Wood

Back row (left to right) - Clyde and Phyllis Wood, Ralph and Maxine Wood, Clara and Bruce Wood, Doris and Lloyd Chaloupka, Lucille and Ralph Neal

Chapter 7

It's a Boy!!

I am told Mom nearly died during my birth. She stayed nearly three weeks recovering in the General hospital in Des Moines. According to my baby book I weighed eight pounds, three and one-half ounces at birth. More than likely, Dad was driving Grandpa's car back and forth 50 miles to Des Moines on country roads. There was no interstate 80 or paved side roads in 1946. U.S. Highway 6 was the main east-west road at the time.

Norma Jean's Dad never did really care for his new son-in-law in their first years of marriage. Dad said he heard his father-in-law say at the hospital, that he, Arden, did not seem to care what happened to Norma Jean. Dad felt he was in a no-win situation with chores to do, new baby pigs, and a father-in-law criticizing him.

One evening Dad had to drive the 50 miles home to do the chores. After chores he had to go throughout the community to find blood donors for Mom's required blood transfusion. With the help of another farmer, they found 18 people willing to sacrifice their next day in Des Moines.

It turned out that three of the eighteen had Mom's blood type. As you might imagine this was a unique group of people who could spend a whole day in Des Moines in the middle of the work week. The three donors were a minister's wife, the town drunk, and a fellow who had been told not to come to their church again. He was a bad influence on the congregation.

Mom came home thinking she might never be able to give birth again. Who knew that four more boys would be born into this family. They came along every other year after this first challenging birth. This new family of three lived with Arden's parents until 1950.

For some reasons probably related to control and pride, Dad chose to leave this seemingly financially sound arrangement, and moved his young family thirty miles southwest to an 80-acre farm west of Fontanelle, Iowa. This land was hilly and rocky, much poorer land by any farmer's standards.

To his dying day, Dad was sure that it was God's will for Mom and him to move to this new farm, 4.5 miles west of Fontanelle. I am not questioning God's will or Dad's interpretation of God's will in this book. Only Dad and Mom could make that call.

Mom and Dad lived long lives, being married 70 years. All five boys graduated from Bridgewater-Fontanelle (B-F) High School. They have since married, raised families, and made a respectable living in their chosen professions.

Some 36 years after my high school graduation, at the age of 54, I went back and biked some of the gravel roads northwest of Fontanelle near our original 80-acre farm. It was exciting riding the mile to the country school again. I was thankful for bike gears, and being in reasonably good biking shape. The hills were every bit as steep as I had remembered them. It was a thrill topping large hills and taking in the old views.

Our farm seemed strangely different, although the same ponds, hills, and terraces were still there. The new house Dad and my brothers had built after I left for college, was already showing its age. The old barn we had worked and played in had been torn down. Al and Jim Walters' house down the hill from us was gone.

I went west past Dean Brown's farm and Hump Conley's farm. My how those farms had changed. The county had quit maintaining the dirt road between our farms. I rode by brother Carroll's farm. There was no one home. Many other houses in the neighborhood had been torn down, or were in a bad state of repair, and sat empty.

I could not get over how quiet it was in the middle of the day. It was spooky in fact. This was a sunshiny day and I expected to see farmers out working in their fields. I looked forward to hearing tractors groaning as they pulled large pieces of farm equipment. I found out most of the farmers, still in our old neighborhood, were working at jobs in town. For many, farming had become their second occupation.

I rode past Richard Edsall's farm and on to Highway 92. In Fontanelle, I took in the remodeled high school, the new, improved athletic complex, the town square, and then rode out to the cemetery east of town. I have always found comfort in cemeteries. The Fontanelle cemetery is full of last names I am very familiar with. Many, some my age, had died way too young. What a day of emotions. What a day of memories.

Four oldest Wood brothers

Front row (left to right) - Dean and Larry
Back row (left to right) - Carroll and Keith

Three youngest Wood brothers

Left to right - Dean, Marvin, and Larry

Mom's 80ᵗʰ Birthday Party

Front row (left to right) - Arden and Norma Jean
Back row (left to right) - Keith, Carroll, Marvin, Dean, and Larry

Chapter 8

The Five Wood Boys

No one wanted to bring May baskets to the Wood house. That was an old tradition in our farm community. Classmates delivered a decorated box or cone of candy on May 1st. These generous guests brought these goodies to your doorstep, yelled 'May Basket', and ran before people in the house could catch them. The Wood boys always had at least one lookout. We loved the challenge. It was like a jail break. They never had a chance.

When Trick or Treat night came around, we took it seriously. You had better have a treat available for the Wood boys. I really think Dad enjoyed it as much as anyone. One night a neighbor was not home when we came in our scarey outfits. Dad found some baling wire and baling twine. We proceeded to tie every door we could find shut. We wired their tractor steering wheels to the drivers' seats. We hung tin cans from their front door. That was way more fun than unwrapping a tootsie roll pop.

Most of the weekly shopping was done in the local towns of Fontanelle, population 750, or Bridgewater, population 250. For school clothes we had to go to the county seat of Greenfield, population 2,500. On rare occasions, some or all of the Wood boys were taken to the big cities of Creston and Atlantic.

In every one of those towns I knew where the stores were that had the ball gloves. I had to try each one on and hit them with my fist to see how they would handle a baseball. Every so often I would ask one of my parents if we could buy this or that glove. I don't ever remember getting a positive answer to that question.

I remember one day I was walking down the street in Creston window shopping. I was going by a hardware/plumbing store. There in the front window was one of my brothers trying out a new bathroom stool, seated there like he was in the outhouse at home.

John Deere Customer Appreciation Day was a big day for the Wood boys. They would take place in the Bridgewater Elementary school gym. The local John Deere dealer would show films of the latest equipment to the local farmers that gathered. If that wasn't thrilling enough, the dealer had lots of brochures you could take home and study later. Those new tractors always looked so powerful and freshly painted.

But the real highlight of the day was a big cattle water tank filled with ice and soda pop. It was there just for the taking. One day I had six bottles of pop: Coca-Cola, Root Beer, Orange and Grape Nehi. What a treat for young boys who hardly ever got pop. John Deere days stopped in Bridgewater somewhere along the line. It may have well been the Wood boys who did them in.

We boys have done lots of things together. The years have taken us to different communities along Interstate 80. Our homes in Iowa range from Bettendorf in the east to the Adair area in the west. We thoroughly enjoy our noisy discussion and competitive cards just as in earlier years. It is probably safe to say, we, along with our wives, are ready to return to our respective quiet homes after all the catching up.

As the 'Wood Boys' prepared for Dad's funeral, we were sharing life experiences with the presiding minister. It was sweet reminiscing about the fun things we had been through together. Playing cards over the years was the common experience we related to most with our stories.

I have been told it is amazing how little siblings know of each others growing up years. I am more convinced of that now. I don't know if Larry, Dean or Marvin ever milked a cow by hand. Marvin, the youngest, was allowed to go out for all high school sports and participate in any other school activities he chose. Dad attended a lot of Dean's and Marvin's games. I don't think Dad ever saw me play a game of anything in high school. In fact, he apologized to me for that very thing in later years.

As for myself and Carroll, the next oldest son, we were busy most of the time as we got older, and were deemed able to milk the 10 dairy cows. We started out early milking cows by hand. It was a challenge just to sit on that little stool and generate the strength needed to get milk in a pail that was about as big as we were.

Sometime within the next five years, Dad purchased two Surge milking machines. That was a big improvement from a young boy's perspective. I believe Mom was relieved of most of her milking duties when the new milk machines were operating properly. In my mind, Mom, Carroll and I were the main milking team with Dad stepping in when needed. Dad was busy at something else such as caring for chickens, feeding pigs, and haying cattle. I know personally I always felt more at ease when Dad and I were working in two separate places.

The worst job of all was milking cows in the cold of winter. We had to keep carrying buckets of hot water from the house to the barn. This water was used to clean the cows udders to prepare for milking. Their bags were in varying degrees of cleanliness depending on whether they had slept in some manure or not. This was true even with the new milk machines. Within five to ten minutes, the water became too cold to put your hands in.

One morning I went back to sleep after Dad had awakened me to milk the cows. It was tough crawling out from under those warm covers onto a cold wood floor. Dad was not real understanding when he came back a second time. I am not sure what happened that day, but Dad was not one to spare the rod. No son of his was going to be spoiled.

The cows had to be milked each morning before school, and within a couple hours after returning home from school. If we were visiting relatives, we had to leave earlier than most of the other families, as those cows needed to be milked.

During summer, there were flies everywhere. We had fly strips hanging from the rafters above the milk cows. They filled up rather regularly with unsuspecting flies. What was dangerous for us was the cows using their tails to keep the flies off. More than a few cows got swatted for hitting us. Mom sometimes offered us a penny for every ten flies we killed in the house. We saw that as easy money.

Probably the high spot of milking was the cheap Zenith radio that played while we worked. Dad pretty much let us pick what we wanted to listen to. I remember each night during the week listening to the Lone Ranger, Our Miss Brooks, and Fibber McGee and Molly. At all other times, we listened to the top 40 musical hits of the day.

I'm sure Larry, Dean, and Marvin gathered and packed lots of eggs. That was a never ending job as far as we brothers were concerned. We all knew how to drive tractors and pick up bales. Dad pushed us all to get out there and earn some money working for neighbors. The other four boys tell me they put up lots of hay after I left home. They worked as teams with two tractors and two lowboys.

We all knew how to pick up rocks, walk the corn for weeds, cut thistles from the pasture, build fences, and fill the manure spreaders. One day Dad and I were pitching chicken manure together, one of my least favorite jobs. Dad said to me, "If you don't learn to work harder than that, you will never be able to hold a job." Although I know that was just Dad talk, sometimes I am suspicious I am still trying to impress Dad with my work ethic.

Learning to work has served the five Wood brothers well. If you want something done call on the Wood boys. They do know how to work. Even as we all begin to retire, we all are still working part-time at something. And for some reason we rarely are volunteers. We need to be earning some money. Who knows when the next depression will hit?

Country School House (note boy's outhouse in lower left)

Country School Picture - 1954

Front row (left to right) - Steve Campbell, Carroll Wood, Chalene Queck, Don Bohling, Ronnie Green, and Diane Wiggins

Middle row (left to right) - Cathy Green, Dean Wiggins, Susan Queck, Wayne Bohling, Marilyn Miller, Steve Lahey, and Keith Wood

Back row (left to right) - Bobbie Dale Green, Max Wiggins, Gerald Queck, Virgil Baudler, Ruth Baudler, Jeanette Miller

Chapter 9

Country School Days

It is funny what you remember about your youth after all these years. I remember looking forward to country school starting, with a new box of 24 Crayola crayons, a new Lone Ranger tablet, and my new Roy Rogers lunchbox. What a thrill it was to have new, unbroken crayons and a new pencil box with new pencils.

Our lunch box always had a sandwich of peanut butter and jelly, or a slice of bologna between two slices of that wonderful, store bought, Wonder Bread. Mom usually got 10 loaves for a dollar at the day-old store. We boys knew it had to be good because as the commercials said, "It builds strong bodies 12 ways".

My brothers and I would take out on our bikes as fast as we could go. It was just a little over a mile up and down hills, that frankly were scary as I look at them today. We would have lunch buckets and ball gloves hanging off the handle bars. We had no bike safety equipment, no bike helmets. Older bikes had long since lost their fenders and chain guards. There was no safety equipment for bike riders. Bike accessories were things like baseball cards in the spokes to make noise. Bike safety equipment just was not thought about even by the most caring mother.

After all, you could always wash off those scrapes, put on some mercurachrome and bandages as needed. The loose gravel roads provided 'strawberries' that lasted weeks. You were always comforted with the words, "Skin grows back, it will heal quickly", and it did as we five boys could attest.

There were usually three hard tire tracks on those gravel roads to ride on, until the road grader came and pushed all the gravel back to the center of the road. Then after a couple of days all that loose gravel would work its way back to the side of the road, and the bike riders were back to full speed.

For all the fun, and anticipation of fun at school, what I remember most are the times I embarrassed myself. There were probably about 15-20 kids going to this one room school, grades K-8. I don't remember one other thing about my first year of school except that early in the year I wet my pants. There was this big puddle under my desk. What was I going to do with it? Who could I blame? And what about the wet clothing. They say a body in shock shuts down. I can vouch for that. I do not remember a thing after I was fingered for the mess.

There were two one-hole outhouses just to the west of the school. All you had to do was raise one finger or two to let the teacher know you needed to use those facilities. I do not know if I was sure enough of myself to negotiate an outhouse. I am quite sure I never had another puddle under my seat.

As a side note, these outhouses were pushed over regularly on Halloween nights. That was pretty standard practice throughout the county. Rumor had it that every so often the outhouses were moved back about three feet before 'trick or treating' started. It may have been parents who started that rumor. As much as you might be suspicious, I can guarantee you I was not involved in such escapades, or even thought about it.

I was not aware of any real discipline problems at the country school. Most fathers were probably like mine. They told us if the teacher ever had to punish us at school we would get punished twice as much when we got home. I did not doubt my father's words, or test his resolve on this issue. I imagine he was just passing along what his father had said to him, and his father before that.

There was a big pot-bellied stove in the center of this one room. Older boys were usually given the task of bringing in coal to keep the stove working efficiently during the winter. Another student job was getting a fresh bucket of water from the hand pump outdoors. There was one good sized metal water dipper that we all drank from and threw water on the person behind us who was prodding you to hurry up.

Still another job was cleaning the blackboard and dusting the erasers outdoors. I faintly remember this job was often reserved for anyone who got in trouble during the day and had to stay after school.

There was a recitation bench right next to the teacher. Different groups of people were called up to recite for the teacher what they had learned in any particular subject. Math was always my best subject. I always did well in math without working all that hard.

My worst subject was reading. I just could not get into reading. Reading always took time away from playing ball or riding bikes. The stories to my mind were all too long and boring. I can still remember the day I decided I would fake reading a story. I would skip all that boring reading. I would just fake the answers for Mrs. Markman, my teacher, when we were called on to recite. Needless to say that did not go well for me. But, unfortunately, that lesson about taking shortcuts continued to be a problem.

If I decided some school work was not all that important, quite often I would find a short cut to complete the task. We had one book in our country school library, entitled, "Too Big". It was a 15-20 page book with big print and big pictures. Every time we had to write a book report you can guess which book I checked out.

I was part of an unusually large class of four: Marilyn Miller, Susan Queck, Dean Wiggins and myself. We were right there together through our six years before the country school closed. My guess is I ranked 3rd in this class of four scholars.

I am not sure why I waited until the end to tell you that we played ball at recess whenever the weather permitted. School buildings were set in one corner of an acre of land. Ball diamonds had to be fit into that acre wherever they could be. An outhouse might well be a base. There was a lot of ball chasing on the other side of the fence. In fact we played cross out, which meant if you could throw the ball between the runner and the base, they were out.

I loved playing ball. I loved to win when playing ball. I am not sure what other players might have said about this young boy's attitude, but I am pretty sure it was not good. I would get upset when the ball game went badly for my team. I would get upset if a teammate struck out. I would get upset when teammates made errors. I am not sure how big of a fuss I made. The teacher was usually too busy to come out and police ball games, or correct bad attitudes. It still embarrasses me to think what I must have been like. Then again, I was a great sport as long as I was winning.

School buildings were also the social center of the community. Potlucks were held there. Card parties were assembled there. Kids played outside in warm weather and inside in the winter. I still remember when I was in sixth grade, the girls came up to me and asked if they could kiss me. I guess it was like practice kissing. Well, what do you do with an offer like that? I took off running, which seemed kind of silly as I thought about it, so I tripped myself.

In recent years, I have gone back to walk around that acre of land. For a while, the school housed a farm combine with an auger protruding out of a window. More recently, the old school house has been torn down, and the land reverted back to just another acre of a hay field. There were a lot of memories wrapped up in that acre of land.

Keith on his bicycle

Chapter 10

Home Field Advantage

There were a lot of ball games played in our barn yard. Our barn yard was about the size of a respectable infield. And it would have been great except for more than a few obstacles. The barn itself was the backstop behind home plate. The corn crib was right behind first base and all along the first base line. The corn crib was great for returning balls thrown toward first. We played what we called cross out. The corn crib was great for returning those throws.

Continuing on around the infield, the yard light pole kept the shortstop from ranging too far to the left. In short center field the black Chevy was parked. In deeper left field was a great big shade tree that provided shade for putting the cultivator on the tractor in summer, or for plucking chickens whenever the meat supply was getting low.

Right down the third base line was one of the few places you could hit without possibly hitting an obstruction. The only trouble was that just a little behind third was the gravel road that ran south of our house. The ditch on the far side of the road was rarely mowed. I can not even estimate how many hours we spent looking for balls that went into that ditch, or the farm field behind it. We finally made the rule if you hit a fly ball into the farm field you were out.

The infield itself had a nice thick layer of rock. You could buy a load of rock from the county and they would deliver it. The traffic-smoothed surface wasn't that bad unless some big service truck pulled in the barnyard and left ruts. Bad hops were more the rule than the exception. Did I mention that if a ball hit the electric line and came down, you could catch it for an out? The same was true if the ball came off the car or the house or fell out of the shade tree.

The land behind the yard light started a gradual, uphill incline, until you came to the pear tree. The pear tree was on the same level plane as our old, two story house, located in straight away center field. There were three steps up to the house about 10 yards behind 2nd base. Usually the car was parked close to those steps.

Around the house were various trees and shrubs. On the left hand corner of the house, between second base and the shortstop position, was an old spirea bush, that may have never been trimmed, in its entire life. It was a beauty. For some reason a lot of our family pictures were taken in front of that spirea plant. As I see those pictures today, I can't help but think of the Goad family in the "Grapes of Wrath".

In right field, or deep second base, was a good sized tree which served as the starting point for a row of lilac bushes going deeper into right field. The lilacs smelled good in the spring. During the rest of the year they were just more of the untrimmed foliage. Trimming plants did not make Dad's 'to do' list. Trimming plants did not put any food on the table. Washing the car fell into the same category.

Deep right field at the end of the row of lilacs was the tool shop and the attached two-hole outhouse. Some of my best hits were over the outhouse and into the orchard behind it. Play stopped after a hit like that, and every player went to look for the ball in the ankle high grass of the orchard. There was really no chance of catching a ball in right field since that was also where the hand water pump and the clothes line were permanently located.

Sometimes Dad might join us for a ball game, making for two teams of three. Most often it was my youngest brother, Marvin, and I taking on brothers Larry and Dean. For some reason Carroll was willing to forgo a lot of this fun. There was probably a Western on TV. On weekends, I might call all the neighborhood boys, and we would have a big game. I was usually the initiator of these games.

Now it is time to tell you about our ball equipment. Dad and Mom did not think hard earned food money should be spent on bats and gloves. I always coveted other boys good balls, bats, and gloves. We had two relatively cheap, flat gloves. They would have been better bases than ball gloves. Kids did not always have their own glove. When the teams changed sides they passed their gloves to the other team.

The ball we used was a semi-hard rubber ball that bounced pretty well but came apart way too soon. After a while the ball would get a divot in it, and another, and another. Shortly, it was time for a new ball which seemed like a big expense to five young boys. I think the use of the rubber ball was necessitated by broken house windows and the safety of the base runners who were being crossed out.

If we had one of our big neighborhood games in an open field, we used a baseball. A new baseball was a treasure for us. I remember Dad taking us to the ball field in town to look for baseballs someone might have lost or left behind. It was a treasure hunt as far as I was concerned. Even as I got older, having a family of my own, Dad would still come up to me and hand me a baseball he had found somewhere. To keep my end of the bargain I thanked him every time. The little boy in me still loved a new baseball.

We had three bats over the years. The easiest to describe was a plain brown bat Dad had picked up at a garage sale. It was not taped anywhere. The second bat was a broken bat that had been left behind at the high school baseball field. We took it home, glued it, put a wood screw in it, and wrapped the break with friction tape.

The third bat we had was split along the grain, length wise. That called for more glue and friction tape, in three places along the barrel of the bat. I still have this third bat hanging in my garage today, just for old times sake. I want to be ready in case any of the neighborhood kids knock on my door to play ball. I am sure the bat is pretty valuable since it was left in the trash 60 years ago.

To complete the equipment story, before I went into high school I bought a new baseball glove. I used my own haying money. To my mind I needed it for high school baseball. It cost me $35. I loved that glove. If we ever went to the basement because of an impending storm I took my ball glove with me.

Dad was upset with me for spending so much money on a ball glove. But he might as well have saved his breath, because that glove was my valued treasure. To this day when I go to a sporting goods store, the first place I go is to the ball glove aisle. I want to see, and smell, and touch, and pound my fist into those new ball gloves.

Now I finally have the money to buy any of those new gloves, but not the arm strength to throw the ball across the infield. However, just in case, I have three ball gloves in my bedroom dresser, that I would have given my left arm for when I was twelve years old. When are those kids going to come to my door and ask me to play ball?

Chapter 11

Time to Eat

Let me start with an oft used farm quote, "Call me anything you want, just don't call me late for lunch." I can't remember a meal where we did not sit down and eat as a family. When it was meal time, you were there. Not that anyone wanted to skip meals or diet. We five boys ate like there was no tomorrow. I call that our depression mentality. And yet, I can remember aunts and uncles commenting, that after all our eating, they still could count each one of us boys' ribs.

If you put it on your plate, you were to eat it. Prompting the well known phrase, "His eyes were bigger than his stomach". I remember the day I did not finish my oatmeal for breakfast. The bowl of oatmeal was put in the refrigerator. Before I was to eat anything else I had to finish that bowl of cold oatmeal. Even today I can not face a bowl of oatmeal.

I can never remember going away from the table hungry. There were always ways to add to the meal if need be. Anything left over could be put on bread for the final course. We ate bread and gravy, bread covered with corn, bread with ketchup on it, and bread with sugar on it.

I thought salmon soup and watery vegetable soup were soups everyone ate. Bring on the saltine crackers. I believe we had popcorn most every night after supper.

Having said all that, I would love to have another plate of Mom's fried chicken, with mashed potatoes and gravy made from the grease. Oh, and throw in some of Mom's homemade rolls to clean up the gravy. When the chicken plate was passed you'd better not be sleeping. By the second time around, the legs and thighs were all gone.

Mom and Dad bought a lot of things in bulk just because it was cheaper. I can remember seeing boxes with 100 hot dogs in them. There was a whiting fish they bought in boxes the same size. They bought boxes of fruit, holding six, one gallon cans. Cereal came in the biggest boxes or bags available. We never had a problem with food spoiling.

Somewhere I learned that when food was provided outside the home I was to eat my fill and then some. At family reunions, Dad would say, eat up boys. It is a long time until supper, and we did.

In junior high, we got school lunches for maybe 35 cents a meal. They would give you as many hot dogs as you wanted. I can remember eating five and six hot dogs with mustard and ketchup on white buns. It makes me groan to even think about it today.

Once a week Mom would bake. We had a big flour container that fit right into the kitchen cabinets. That was one job Mom tried to include the boys in, if we wanted to help. I am sure we were a big help. It seemed we had flour everywhere. Mom would make 3 to 5 loaves of homemade bread, a big pan of homemade rolls, and another big pan of cinnamon rolls.

Finally, whatever bread dough was left over was rolled out on a cookie sheet and covered with cinnamon and sugar. That was our baking day treat. We ate it as soon as it had cooled. We had to wait for a regular meal to eat the frosted cinnamon rolls. It still makes me laugh to think we boys thought the real treat was having Wonder Bread from the store.

Gardens and orchards did a lot to supplement the food supply. Creamed asparagus was great as long as it lasted. Creamed peas and new potatoes went fast at the table. I ate a lot of ripe tomatoes for snacks, using a salt shaker to add flavor.

It was some good eating when the sweet corn was ripe. Dad had to act quickly before the raccoons discovered the ripe corn. Watermelons and cantaloupes were always a big hit. And when the fruit trees produced, we boys were out sampling the fruit. We were expected to hoe and weed in the garden to help Mom out. Mom used us sparingly to pick strawberries. There were a lot of strawberries that never made it into the house.

Mom always canned or froze any food we did not eat as it ripened. Canning was a tough job, in a hot kitchen, even with every window open. We boys got to help pick and prepare fruit, snap beans, pick tomatoes and remove peas from their pods. Digging the last of the potatoes and storing them in the basement ended the garden season. All canned foods were stored in the cellar under our house.

I have always enjoyed daily physical exercise. That may be the only thing that saved me from gaining lots of weight over the years. Eating more than I needed has been an unfortunate bad habit. I just never knew when I might be forced to skip a meal, or when the next depression may hit.

Chapter 12

Before Indoor Plumbing

I grew up about the time families were putting bathrooms inside their houses. What a pleasant change that was. Up until that time, each family had what they called an outhouse. It might have one seat or two. Ours had two, but I do not recall ever sharing the facility with someone.

The outhouse often had a crescent moon carved into the upper part of the bathroom door. The Sear's catalog was an important accessory. It was used both for perusing during the visit, and as toilet paper at the end. During cold weather one did not dawdle much over the reading material. On warm summer days, these facilities put out a pungent odor.

Every so often, Dad brought the manure spreader around and did some house cleaning, by removing the lower door in the back of the outhouse. I really can't remember if I ever had to do that job. It wasn't that big of a deal compared to cleaning out pig lots, chicken houses, cow barns and lots. It is amazing that all this manure is great for growing crops. Dad relied on manure instead of buying fertilizer.

We boys always made sure Dad knew how terrible those jobs were, but we might as well have been talking to the wind. I remember us putting bandanas over our noses to lessen the smell. Looking back, I am pretty sure the bandanas were more symbolic than functional.

Five boys did not always go to the outhouse to relieve themselves. Any good tree or just stepping behind the barn provided the necessary privacy. It was way too far to the outhouse. At night there was always a chamber pot in the hallway on the second floor.

Well, I'm guessing you have learned way more than you wanted to know about the Wood outhouse. I will close with one of Dad's favorite stories, "Did you know that John Deere makes a product they won't stand behind? It's true. They won't stand behind their manure spreaders."

Chapter 13

Country Church, Highland Methodist

The Highland Methodist Church was seven miles northeast of the family farm. There were probably eight pews on each side of the center aisle. There was an overflow room with two more pews. I would say there were between 30 and 50 people in attendance on any given Sunday in 1960.

In preparation for church, we had Saturday night baths. Although more frequent baths might have been ideal, that was our routine. And everyone used the same bathwater, so it was a blessing to be one of the first bathers. One other Saturday night task was polishing your shoes for church. During my younger years we wore the same shoes for chores and for church. A little cleaning and some brown liquid shoe polish did the trick.

Church service started when the choir came in two by two, singing "Onward Christian Soldiers". Every choir member had an assigned green choir robe. Mom and Marvin were the only members of our family who sang well enough to earn one of those robes.

Because the church was so small, it took two churches to support a minister. Our pastor, Reverend Eshelman, preached at

Highland after preaching at the Fontanelle Methodist Church. He was a faithful servant and a fine example of a Christian man.

We adolescent boys always sat in the second and third rows on the right. We thought we were being independent sitting by ourselves. Our parents liked that arrangement, as they could watch our behavior during the service.

In the era of mega-churches and multimedia worship services, it is hard to picture a church where everyone is just a faithful servant, lots of good farm families joining together to worship. I don't remember a Sunday when our family missed church, except for really bad weather. Besides the chores and three meals prepared by Mom, our family never did any work on Sunday.

The rural population declined. Due to the age and size of the congregation it was decided to close the church. A service to celebrate the church was held on September 28, 2008. Mom, Dad, my four brothers, and I attended that service. It was one of the most tearful, happy homecomings I have ever attended. The church was packed with past members. Within the year, the building was demolished and the property restored to agricultural use. It had housed this congregation 110 years.

Chapter 14

Television Comes to the Wood House

The first TV show I saw was at a neighbor's house. It was some kind of suspense thriller, that had me really scared. I was probably between eight and ten at the time.

Our family's first television was a 25" Zenith black and white. We got the TV as sort of a family Christmas present. There were few other gifts that year. I remember feeling very disappointed with the homemade sock-puppet I received.

Because we lived 60 miles from both Des Moines and Omaha the reception was always bad. We used rabbit ears, with aluminum foil attached, to try to improve the reception. Sometimes it even worked.

There were only three channels possible in southwest Iowa. The channels came out of Des Moines, Omaha, and Ames. Remote controls did not exist. The TV had basically two dials of any value, the off/on switch, and the channel changer. TV tubes might burn out and could be replaced at an electronics store.

I remember, while in high school sitting in an easy chair, watching TV, listening to the St. Louis Cardinals baseball game on radio, and doing my math homework all at the same time. That may help explain my fine study habits when I went off to college.

The favorite shows for our family were, "Andy Griffith" on Monday night, "Red Skelton" on Tuesday night, and "I Love Lucy" on Wednesday night. On Saturday night we got to stay up later. That was the night for "Gunsmoke" and "All-Star Wrestling". Every so often 'The Ed Sullivan Show', on Sunday night, would have some big attractions, like Elvis Presley, or the Beatles.

"All-Star Wrestling" featured good guys like Vern Gagne and Haystack Calhoun. The good guys were rare among many villainous wrestlers. The crowds, prompted by cue cards, would cheer and boo depending on the action. Body slams, airplane spins, and jumping on your opponent from the top rope, were some of the wrestling moves you might see.

Then they would have a tag-team match that was even crazier. The evil wrestler outside the ring would often sneak into the ring, and it would be two against one. The good guys trying to be fair would really take a beating before the referee finally stepped in. It seems there was always an older lady in the front row who was really upset. She would often come up near the ring and hit a villain with her purse. Young boys were impressed with all this action.

All TV was pretty safe during those days. Parents did not have to worry about their kids watching shows that were too explicit. "All-Star Wrestling" may have been the most violent show on TV. In the many westerns the guys in white hats always prevailed. In the sit-coms families were model families and each show had a moral to be learned.

Chapter 15

Wood Family Cards

It has been said if you want to have a good time, go play cards with the Wood boys, however, not everyone says that. After the five boys' honeymoons were over, no daughter-in-law has ever come into the card playing room.

Although all players are around the same table, you would think at least some of the players were hard of hearing. Loud talking is a must. How can you insult opponents in a quiet voice? Heaven forbid that your opponent might not hear just how poorly he played that hand.

Such phrases as "watch and learn" and "should we change partners and give the other team a chance?" have come out of these discussions. Getting to 50 first in Ten Point Pitch is of course the objective, but it is equally important that you educate your opponents, or they might make the same mistake again.

One of the principles you learn right away is that getting the bid is crucial, in fact it is of much higher concern than going set on your bid. If you bid low for some crazy reason, brother Larry will groan and direct you to, "Go sit in the corner and turn your face to the wall."

Another rule you learn sooner than you might imagine is that a game ends when the losing team goes 50 in the hole. Those facing such a dilemma might be quoted as saying, "Sicker calves than this have gotten well."

Ten Point Pitch has 3 variations: 1) Two teams, with either 4 or 6 players wanting to play, 2) three teams of 2 with 6 players, and 3) the infamous call for your partner when an odd number of players are gathered around. In this later game a bid of less than 8 will be scoffed at. A bid of ten is not unusual, nor is the subsequent set.

As the game proceeds some person or team decides it's time to make a move and they 'shoot the moon'. With this 'do or die' tactic the bidding team either makes 50 points or loses 50 points. More than likely this tactic will end the game. No matter how this game goes there is a lot of teaching and learning that takes place at the conclusion. But what the heck, draw a line on the score sheet, shuffle the cards and we are off to the next game.

Some of the fault goes back to our Grandpa Wood. He loved to have families visit and play cards. He was determined to win. If he would happen to lose 2 out of 3 games, we were automatically playing 3 out of 5, or 4 out of 7, as need be. No Wood cousin ever remembers Grandpa taking it easy on them because they were young and easily hurt.

More than a few times neighbors came over to play cards without even calling ahead, or Dad might say, "Let's go over to so-and-so's house and play some cards." Everyone was free to bring in a guest to our house without prior notice. My choice for a guest was J.C. McCall, a classmate of mine. He always seemed to fit right in, taking his sets, with a big smile on his face.

When people were leaving after a night of cards, Dad would say, "Come back again when you learn to play a little better". Guests would laugh and wave goodbye as they pulled out of the yard, and they would come back when they needed a break from the routine of life. Mom always had that big bowl of popcorn ready when they did return. Playing cards, feeling comfortable, having fun, and rowdy laughter all seemed to go together.

Chapter 16

Early Farm Tractors

If there was a positive side to farming, it was driving farm tractors. I was always glad when my job for the day was mowing hay, or side-raking hay, or plowing, or disking the newly plowed ground, or cultivating corn. It was exhilarating being out in open fields, just you and a powerful tractor. In warm spring and summer days we would take off our shirts to get that good farmer tan. My skin doctor tells me that we farm kids will continue to pay for our worship of the sun.

As much as I loved to drive farm tractors, they were not user-friendly for young boys. Our F-20 Farmall was made for a man to operate. As a youngster I could either sit on the front of that hard old metal seat and steer, or I could slide off and stand on the metal platform the seat was attached to.

Someone had to start the engine of the F-20 with a hand crank. Dad usually did that job. It was great when the engine turned over the first time. That was rare. Depending on how well the engine was tuned, you might have to crank several times to get the engine going.

The real challenge for a young boy was getting the tractor started and stopped. The clutch had to be pushed clear in with your left leg. Then the brakes had to be applied. with the right leg. Pushing both the clutch and the brake forward at the same time proved an impossibility for short legged boys. Dad had hand clutches and hand brakes installed on our tractor so we boys could handle stopping and starting again.

These tasks got easier over the years, as we grew, and as we got newer, more user-friendly tractors. During my high school years we had two 'WD' Allis-Chambers. They seemed very modern compared to the old F-20. Most tractors had push button starters by that time.

I considered myself an accomplished tractor driver as I got older. I could back a two-wheeled low-boy of hay through most any opening in a shed, and with two or three tries I could back a four-wheeled wagon pretty close to where I wanted it.

The earliest harvesting job I remember, on the farm was harvesting oats with a threshing machine in either 1954 or 1955. One farmer in the area, owned a treshing machine. He would go from farm to farm with this big machine. He pulled it with his huge tractor, which would in turn provide the power to run the threshing machine. It had a long belt about a foot wide that ran between the tractor and the threshing machine, probably 10 yards apart.

Area farmers would help each other bringing bundles (shocks) of oats from the fields to the threshing machine. My job was to take a water jug to the farmers as they brought their wagon loads of oats to the threshing machine. Harvesting oats that way was such a hot, dirty job. Everyone in the area of the threshing machine took a bath as soon as possible in the evening.

In recent years I have gone back to help Carroll pick corn on his farm. His farm is about a mile west of where Dad's original 80-acre farm was located. I got to haul loads of corn right past our original homestead. Carroll's two tractors, though not new, were new to me. They are big John Deeres, that are quite an improvement over the older models I learned on. It is a big step up, sitting inside an air-conditioned tractor cab with the radio playing.

How thrilling it was pulling loads of corn over the very same roads we boys had ridden our bikes on, going to country school. It just so happens that Carroll rented the land where our old country school was located. I had time to walk around that country school acre of land, now just a hay field.

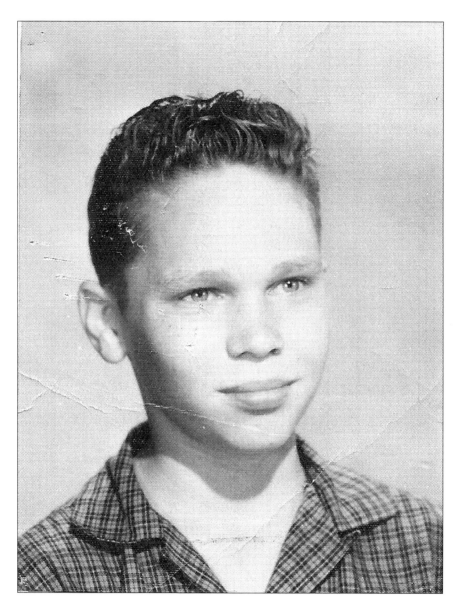

Keith - 8th Grade Picture

Chapter 17

Those Teen Years

At the Arden Wood household there was not a lot of pampering. Our parents had not received any coddling when they were young, nor did they pass any along. You were expected to "buck up" and get over any conflicts.

One of Dad's early quotes was, "If you keep crying I will give you something to cry about." Love was assumed but never expressed. Saying, "I love you" was very rare in my parents' generation.

Looking back, I see myself as a high school freshman, in three separate worlds. In the first world, on the farm, I see myself as a confident leader of my younger brothers. In the neighborhood I was the one who called all the neighborhood boys together for an afternoon baseball game.

World number two was Bridgewater-Fontanelle (B-F) High School. I knew about half of my 40 classmates, but not that well. I was content to just fade into the background whenever possible. World number three was avoiding any interaction with adults.

Going back to world number two, I will share with you three incidents that happened to me during the fall of my freshman year of high school. It just so happened that B-F was kind of a 1A football powerhouse in southwest Iowa. In my four years of high school football, I think we lost five games. We were undefeated in both my freshman and senior years.

Unfortunately, the part I played in that great record was small. I weighed 96 pounds as a freshman; 126 pounds as a senior. They had trouble finding football gear small enough to fit me in my freshman year.

I had no idea you had to train that hard just to play a game. Football was a lot easier in the back yard, on the farm. There, I was always the quarterback throwing winning touchdowns. Dad always told me he played football on the starting team, all four years, at his high school, so I just assumed I would do the same. I finally made the kick-off team as a senior.

One incident stands out in my mind even today. It was a cold, late fall football practice. We were having tackling practice. In those days, the whole squad practiced together. At least at times, tackling drills were not separated by grade or size. One line of boys were ball carriers; the opposing line were tacklers. The 100 pound freshmen went up against the 200 pound senior linemen.

On one of my turns I come up against the starting left tackle. I go charging toward him and at the last second I slide to the right and tripped him. I did not plan to do that, it just happened. I can still feel the embarrassment of that moment. The coach had to be chuckling. He sent me back to try it again.

There were several freshmen that year who wondered what they were doing there. Some of the bigger freshman played and did reasonably well. I remember being huddled with Steve Frese and Rick Roberts on a cold night in Adair. Those long warm-up coats were supposed to keep us warm in the wind and the cold. They did not. The coach would have had to thaw me out first, if he had sent me into the game.

The second traumatic experience I endured, was freshman initiation. I think they stopped this ritual shortly after our class went through it. To my mind all the seniors boys were athletic heroes and the girls were the prettiest young ladies I had ever seen. Now these seniors were telling me to come to school the next day dressed as a hula dancer. It was great having all the kids in school laughing at you. That was a long day.

Incident number three was at a dance after a home football game. I did not know how to dance even if I had had the nerve to ask a girl to dance. After the dance Bonnie Euler, the prettiest of the senior girls, in my mind, came up and asked if I had enjoyed the dance. I told her I had not danced. I had just watched. She said to me, "You should have asked me to dance. I would have danced with you".

In my wildest dreams, I could not even imagine that happening. In my mind, she and I were on opposite ends of the social spectrum. There was no way I would be able to put an arm around her, and stand, and breathe all at the same time. I think I just shrugged my shoulders. What could I say?

Things could only go up from there, and they did. I always got good grades. I lettered two years in baseball and a year in football. I was a class officer. I had a girlfriend. Even with that, I never felt I was worthy to be with the "in crowd".

So I have told you about my first world on the farm, and the second world at high school. My third world was life interacting with adults. Dad let us boys know that when he was talking to adults we were not to interrupt him. That was no problem for me, as there were no adults I really desired to talk to except Mom. It was really hard for me to look adults in the eye and talk to them. Dad would get after me for being so shy, but I had no desire to insert myself into his adult world.

Chapter 18

Leaving the Farm — Higher Education

For lack of a better plan, I left the farm to attend Commercial Extension (CE) in Omaha, Nebraska. This was a two-year business school. There were several of us from B-F going there including my girlfriend, Jeanie. A recruiter for the school told us there were ball teams in Omaha, so I was willing to give up my senior year of high school summer baseball. I had $500 saved from years of working for farmers, mostly making hay. It just so happened that was pretty much the tuition for CE.

Six months later, I learned, there was a ball team at CE. I would just have to find the players and organize it. Forget that. Later I learned that a degree from CE would not qualify me to be an accountant. I could get a job as a bookkeeper. One day the president of CE was chewing me out for being late to class. I can remember thinking that was totally uncalled for. The next day I went to the office and dropped out of school. My girlfriend and I had broken up a couple of months earlier.

By the next January, I was enrolled at the University of Northern Iowa (UNI). The time in between is kind of a blur. Dad was not impressed with my decision making. I had gone through my savings and had nothing to show for it. Somehow the proper loan forms were filled out and I was accepted at UNI.

On a cold, windy, and snowy day, the folks dropped me off at Shull Hall on the Cedar Falls campus. The only person I knew there was Rick Roberts, my high school friend and sports buddy. He was in the same hall, but on a different floor and wing. He already had a semester behind him.

I got through that first semester somehow. That was following my skipping freshman orientation. I can't imagine what I was thinking. My adviser signed me up for Analysis II since I told him I had always done well at math. He really did not care. It was up to me. At the end of the semester, I had a 'C-' in Analysis II, and a 'D' in Humanities. Humanities had a textbook the size of a big family dictionary. Needless to say I did not get it all read. I was on probation going into the following year of classes.

That second year I took Calculus and got a 'D'. That prompted my decision to become a business major. I could take some of the business classes I was familiar with from CE and get my grades up. Somehow that logic worked. I enjoyed the college social life and intramural sports. I rarely went home. I worked a lot of hours in the school cafeteria. That was an easy way to make friends, make some money, and the work was easy compared to farming.

I learned to dance, at least enough to meet more girls. That was a big step for me. Slowly, but surely, I was gaining confidence in myself. At least enough to realize I could make it, and enjoy life. I attended summer school to catch up with my class and earn money at the school cafeteria. Each summer I was always part of a fast pitch college softball team. I had pretty well decided college was not that bad. In fact, I really enjoyed my freedom.

Studies got in the way, but they were doable. One semester I even got a 3.25 grade point. By that time I knew I was going to make it at college. Late in my junior year someone brought up the topic of student teaching. The thought kind of startled me. I wasn't sure I even wanted to student teach. I had forgotten that college life had an ending point.

I made it through student teaching in Mason City with a 'C'. That was not good, but it got me past another hurdle. The next shocker came, as it was time to apply for teaching jobs. With all my academic success, I was going to grab the first job offer that came along. Fortunately that offer came from North Scott in Eldridge, Iowa. It was to teach Jr. High Math (my minor) and coach football, wrestling, and track.

Even today I still have a soft spot in my heart for North Scott. When I think about where I might have found my first job I am so thankful North Scott hired me early.

I was excited about the possibilities. I am quite sure I got the job because I was willing to coach wrestling at 6:00 in the morning. There was only one problem; I had zero experience in wrestling. Oh well, I could read about it and learn on the go. Being in over my head had not stopped me before.

One aspect of college that has me a little bewildered is the fact that I had friends all along, but none of them were lasting friends. Only one, Duane Fredrich, corresponded and got me in his baseball pool. My two best friends, Dennis Moeller and

Keith Hicklin, have not corresponded since college. I think I know the cities they live in, but we have never kept in touch.

To me, it just points out how selfish I was during my college years. I enjoyed lots of social events and people, but when it came right down to it, I was all about me. I quit going to church somewhere along the way. I was content being a prodigal son.

The fact that confirms my selfishness most to me is that I hardly ever wrote home. Mom would give me a stack of post cards and say just drop us a note. Dad would get after me to write home. I just could not find the time in my busy social schedule. This fact embarrasses me to this day.

My first year of teaching went well in my estimation. North Scott was a farming community with lots of kids who knew how to work. Every first-year teacher has a lot of work to do to be ready for classes. I did it. I enjoyed the math. I enjoyed the coaching. I even was going to be the assistant high school baseball coach.

Before we had our first baseball game I received my draft notice and was off to basic training in Ft. Lewis, Washington. In the years of the Viet Nam Conflict the Iowa Selective Service would let you teach a year, before they drafted you. That way you had a job waiting for you when you returned from the service.

Chapter 19

You're in the Army Now

It just so happened that a former UNI roommate of mine, Ron Marr, worked at the Army induction center in Omaha, Nebraska. He had been in the Army a couple years by then. He told me if I processed through Omaha, they were sending people to Ft. Lewis, Washington for basic rather than Ft. Leonard Wood in Missouri. From what I had heard of Ft. Leonard Wood, that was a great idea.

I don't know for sure, but I think Ron was able to get me into the dental field as a dental assistant, rather than the random draw that could have well put me in the infantry. I have not located Ron since, but I still thank him.

Next thing I know we new recruits are riding in an Army bus. We are being escorted to our new barracks, along some Ft. Lewis, Washington base street. It is June of 1969. I am now 23 years old. It is a quiet ride with the occasional talking of two recruits, saying "This isn't so bad, I guess."

All of a sudden we turned a corner into a barracks area. Three drill sergeants charged onto the bus, and started calling us names our mothers would not have approved of. Welcome to eight weeks of basic training. We learned to listen up, and obey quickly. If a young private messed up, he was in front of the drill sergeant, completely embarrassed, explaining why he was so incompetent. After a very short discussion, the whole platoon would run and/or do push-ups because we were a team.

There were so many things I did not like about Army life: shaved heads, forever standing in lines, early to bed and early to rise, hurrying to wait, cleaning latrines, pulling KP (helping the cooks), and standing guard duty late at night when no one in their right minds would be up anyway.

More than once, I fell asleep on guard duty and, fortunately, never got reported. On others nights, I was not awakened to do guard duty as the private who was to get me up had fallen asleep. I guess that says we were not losing sleep worrying. The drills and classes during the day were very tiring.

I got good at staying in the background. I did not volunteer for anything. One of my biggest problems was keeping up on quick-paced walks. My short legs just could not keep up with long-legged leaders. I was pleasantly surprised that I was in good physical shape compared to most. I ran a pretty good mile in timed runs.

One of the most satisfying blunders I committed happened one night while we were on a three-day bivouac, out in the wilderness. Two guys were assigned to each tent. During the night there was a surprise, simulated enemy attack. There were ambushes with blank gunfire, soldiers running everywhere, and instructions were given over loud speakers. The next morning many of the fellows in our platoon were grousing around, complaining about being kept up most of the night. My tent mate and I had a big smile on our faces. We had slept through the whole training exercise.

After graduation from basic training, we gathered in a large room to find out what our new MOS (Military Occupation Specialty) was, and what army base we were going to next. This was really a nervous time for all of us, as the Viet Nam Conflict was still going strong. Large groups of names were read and all were told to go to this and that building for further information. The room kept emptying out. I was pretty well the only one left.

A sergeant did some research for me as I still had no direction. He finally came back and told me I was going to be a dental assistant. I was upset at the time, being separated from all the guys I had gotten to know. I was the only person in the room with that MOS. Looking back, what a blessing. Thanks again Ron.

A day or two later I was on my way to Ft. Sam Houston in San Antonio, TX. This was another ten weeks of training. The first two weeks we trained with the medics. The training films showed in full color the types of wounds you would be dealing with. Those two weeks were enough to make me appreciate not being a medic.

Dental Assistant training was great. We wore white smocks each day, like doctors and nurses wear. Going to school was right up my alley. In fact I graduated second in a class of 20 plus men and women. I always liked San Antonio with the river walk, the Alamo, and the Trinity College's Bell Tower. Little did I know that 40 years later, a college soccer tournament in San Antonio would provide me with one of the biggest thrills of my life, as a parent.

I became more and more daring as time passed. One weekend I hitch-hiked up to Killeen, Texas. Brother Carroll and his wife, Linda, were stationed there at Ft. Hood. We played a round of golf and spent some time together. I remember several of my fellow dental students could not believe I would attempt such a thing on a weekend. I had hitch-hiked home from college several times so I had a little experience. Driver's seemed very willing to pick up a soldier in uniform.

My first real duty station was Ft. Campbell, Kentucky. I made some new friends. In fact, I bought a car to get around. The number of my friends increased. I learned that if you stay around the base on the weekends you are likely to get volunteered for some work. Consequently, I took weekend trips to places like the Kentucky Derby, Mardi Gras in New Orleans, and Nashville's country music scene.

During my time at Ft. Campbell, I was able to do on-the-job training (OJT) to become a dental hygienist. This was a nice step up. I now had my own patients, and my own dental chair. I was at Ft. Campbell long enough to enroll for a night class at Austin-Peay University. Unfortunately, I did not get through the semester. Orders came through that I was to serve a year in Viet Nam.

Keith near his barracks in Viet Nam - 1971

934th Dental Detachment – 1971

Keith – Front row, 3rd from right
Jon Dinkle (best friend), over Keith's left shoulder

Chapter 20

The Viet Nam Conflict

I paid so little attention to the news in 1970 that I did not know much about the Viet Nam Conflict. All I knew was, there were a lot of young Americans dying. The evening newsmen always said there were more North Vietnamese dying than Americans. So obviously, we must be winning.

In my writing about this conflict I found it is now called the Vietnam War, so let me shift gears. As I watch documentaries on the Vietnam War today, I see it was a complicated situation. There were way too many political battles going on in Washington D.C. Many of the leaders at the time were more concerned about looking good and getting elected than ending the war. We fought battles that should have never been fought. We would win hills, causing many to lose their lives, and then leave them; only to come back and fight for them again. At the conclusion of all the fighting the goal was not to win but to leave honorably. I do not think we even achieved that.

Our country was deeply divided on whether we should have sent any troops at all. There were many students protesting on college campuses. Many of the returning troops were treated poorly, like it was their fault that the war was dragging on and that people were losing their lives. I arrived back in the states at

3:00 in the morning in May of 1971. There was no one around to meet our flight. That was probably just as well.

I have been told that for every soldier on the front line, there are nine or ten support troops behind him. I was fortunate to be one of the nine or ten. In fact I never even had a weapon assigned to me during the whole tour of duty in Vietnam.

My younger brother, Carroll, had finished his year in Vietnam a year before I went into the service. He was a crane operator who unloaded ammo and equipment from ships coming into Vietnam. The Department of Defense did not allow more than one brother to go to a war zone at any given time.

Poor Mom and Dad had three boys in the Army at pretty much the same time. Brother Larry got stationed in Germany and got to travel all over Europe. He laughs about all the power he had as a company clerk. He was the one who typed up orders for all the men in his unit.

Quentin Coffman and Gene Conrad, my teaching buddies from North Scott, took me to Oakland, California by way of the Grand Canyon, Yellowstone Park, and Disneyland. They were up for a summer trip out West and I enjoyed being with them. It was a great vacation leading into my year-long trip to Vietnam.

It was a long flight to Vietnam leaving from Oakland, California. We stopped and refueled in Hawaii. No one was allowed off the plane. I still remember wondering on the flight over if we would have to seek cover as we got off the plane. Actually it was like landing in any other airport in the states, except you were with a lot of guys who really did not want to be there.

My year of service was spent in a dental clinic in Nha Trang. It was a beautiful place just west of Cameron Bay. If you had to be in Vietnam, it was a good place to be. I am told Nha Trang was an in-country Rest and Relaxation (R&R) site earlier in the war.

There was a nice beach within two miles of our barracks. Nha Trang was located next to the South China Sea. I really enjoyed body surfing as the waves came in. We were able to go snorkeling and have picnics on surrounding islands during the year. Tough duty, huh. If it had not been for the continual threat of war it would have been good duty. Everyone in Vietnam got an extra $50 a month (as I remember it) called hazardous duty pay. There was no getting around it. Some jobs were more hazardous than others.

I had an eight-hour day at the dental clinic, with seven or eight cleaning appointments during each day. Soldiers traveling through Nha Trang for various reasons would make an appointment to have their teeth cleaned. Front line soldiers going through on tanks were not always impressed with our part in the war. In fact they called us names that I shall not print. 'Rear-echelon' was the prefix to whatever they wanted to add. It really was unfair, the different levels of danger that soldiers faced. Many came home with physical and mental problems because of the stress they were under. Others came home addicted to drugs.

I think I was a pretty good dental hygienist. I received many compliments from those I cared for. In fact the army offered me $6,000 to re-enlist for four more years. That was pretty good money at the time. I never really considered staying in the Army. I was ready to be a teacher again and get back to Iowa. Lots of people got similar bonus offers, some even more, depending on their specialty, and what it cost to train a new person to take their place. I'm sure dentists and doctors all got substantial offers.

Movies were available often in the evenings in Nha Trang. Vietnamese bands played American songs. 'California Dreamin' and 'Hey, Hey, Hey, Good-bye' were always favorites. Guys would sing at the top of their lungs. Everyone knew how many days they had left before their tour of duty was up.

Every so often we were told to go to our sandbagged bunkers because there was some incoming fire. I never did really know if we were in danger of enemy fire. I do remember the day our gasoline reservoir got hit. You could see the flames from everywhere in Nha Trang. It burned most of the day.

The scariest incident I had in Vietnam happened while being on guard duty, at the dental clinic. Someone stayed there every night, I guess to avoid the North Vietnamese messing with our dental clinic. On this particular night there were shooting sounds close, and it just went on and on. I don't remember when or how I learned the truth. It just so happened it was the 4th of July. The shots were all fireworks entertaining the troops.

The cockroaches were huge (3 inches) and numerous. Dogs had to be nervous in Vietnam. If they wandered downtown they might be part of the Vietnamese stew the next day. Open sewers made for a smell you just got used to. During the monsoon season it seemed to rain all the time. When the wind came up, the rain blew in horizontally. I remember that the full moons seemed very large there. It was pretty country with Appalachian-like mountains surrounding the city and the military compound.

During my year-long stay I was able to visit dental assistant friends who were stationed in Saigon, the South Vietnamese capital. That was the main area for the real war activities. Jets and helicopters flew in and out of there regularly. Saigon was the big city when compared to small town Nha Trang.

I flew in C-130 planes or helicopters if I had to go very far. It was always a little scary riding in an open helicopter. Machine door gunners were stationed on each side of the helicopter. They fired their machine guns every so often at who knows what. I am pretty sure no one was firing on us.

I also got to take R&R visits to Hong Kong and Sydney, Australia. Hong Kong was fun to explore, but nothing like home. In Australia, I got to stay on a farm for three days. It was so like an American farm that I got homesick for Iowa. I also remember walking around Sydney watching cricket games. There were games at high school, college, and professional levels. These games were enough like our baseball games to make me miss the competition of a good ball game.

In 1971, President Nixon was trying to draw down the troops. The U.S. Government was trying very hard to get out of Vietnam honorably. Because of that effort, I was able to leave Vietnam 40 days earlier than originally planned. With so little time left in the Army, I processed out as soon as I got back to the states.

I had planned to stop and visit Jon Dinkle, my best friend in Vietnam. He lives in a suburb of Los Angeles. He had rotated out a couple months before I did. As the day drew near I realized I could not stop anywhere. I wanted to get home. Mom had written me faithfully all year. I wanted to get home and see her and my family. What a pleasant homecoming. There was one Christmas that was very special. It happened when all of us Wood soldiers were home safely from our military obligations.

Chapter 21

The Summer of Me

In the summer of 1971, the Vietnam War was over for me. I looked up all my old friends, male and female, I had left behind while in the service. Quentin Coffman, my roommate before I left North Scott, was going to summer school at the University of Iowa at Iowa City. That sounded good to me. We rented an apartment. What better place could there be to make up for lost time.

I'm pretty sure I was still a prodigal son in my parents' eyes. I still was not attending church. I was still into any social event that was available. I was still the college student going for the most enjoyment possible. I was now 25 years old and way past the settling down age by my parents' standards.

I had saved up some money from my two years in the service. I was always pretty much a saver. But now I was ready to live. I bought a four-year-old, lime green Mustang convertible with white leather top and interior to escort myself into this new life.

I signed up for a couple college classes at the University of Iowa. It seemed like the thing to do. After reading the syllabus of the first class, I dropped it. The teacher was expecting way too much work. The second class was something like Introduction to School Administration. They were not trying to scare any temporary students off, so I made my way through that. I can guarantee you I was not the top student in the class.

Quentin and I played either tennis or golf most every afternoon. Our skill levels were very comparable, so we enjoyed the time together. If it was real warm, as it usually was, we would buy a whole cold watermelon and devour it under a shade tree. On other days we might order a large malt at the Purple Cow and indulge ourselves. Now this was living. I joined a co-ed softball team. From my perspective, all these young kids were just as selfish and uncaring as I was. After some embarrassing losses, I moved on.

Jon Dinkle, my Army friend from Vietnam, came from California and spent a weekend. We drove to Chicago in my convertible to meet a third Army friend. It was good to see the guys again, but we each had our own lives now, and wanted to leave the war behind. I was certainly not concerned about other people's problems, or investing my life in anything but me.

Chapter 22

A Knock at the Door

For some reason my folks had decided to come visit me, in my Davenport apartment. Their visits were rare. But that was fine as we did not have a lot in common. The 1971 school year had started. I was back at North Scott teaching Jr. High Math, and coaching Jr. High football, wrestling, track, and high school girls softball.

As I walked Mom and Dad around North Scott and showed them my classroom, they seemed to be impressed. North Scott was a pretty large school compared to B-F. Quentin and I had once again rented an apartment in Davenport, on the west side of Bridge Avenue, between Kimberly Road and the cemeteries to the north.

Dad and Mom were having trouble getting comfortable in our bean bag chairs. They were our most comfortable pieces of furniture. It really was hard to play cards around a low table, sitting in bean bag chairs. I had drafted a young lady down the hall to be my partner for a game of 10-point pitch. No doubt the folks and I would enjoy ourselves playing the Wood family game.

Shortly after we started playing, there was a knock on the door. Two young ladies were standing there when I opened the door.

The one girl I knew faintly. She introduced me to a new young lady, Eta, a first year elementary teacher at Pleasant Valley. Eta wanted to join me when I went to play volleyball in the park. Eta was very pretty, and had a big smile. Why sure, I would be willing to take her to the weekly volleyball game.

It just so happened that, earlier in the fall, I had joined a singles group, sponsored by St. John's Methodist Church. Every Tuesday night they had a volleyball game at Vander Veer Park. It was just a fun group who liked to socialize together. Eta would have no trouble fitting in.

What did Mom and Dad think of all this? No doubt they were as shocked as I was. At least they knew I was not holed up somewhere living all alone. I took Eta to volleyball, and anywhere else she would let me take her. One night she took me to her apartment. There she introduced me to her roommate Doris, a first year math teacher at Pleasant Valley Jr. High. She was as pretty as Eta. Where had these girls been all my life?

Any time I was invited, I was over at their apartment, talking with them. All through the summer, after Vietnam, I had been searching for meaning in life. These two girls seemed to have their lives together. They were telling me about the Bible studies they were doing at the time. I knew about the Bible. I had just not attended church very much or read the Bible for several years.

They encouraged me to read my Bible and get to know Jesus better. I started reading the book of John as they recommended. The teachings of the Bible, and the person I saw in Jesus were making sense.

For some reason, Eta began encouraging me to start dating Doris. I am not sure, either Doris, or I, were all that excited about the possibility. But within the month, Doris and I were enjoying spending time together. Living across the street from each other made it handy to get together in the evenings.

We were certainly from different backgrounds. Her family lived in Clinton, Iowa and were very quiet by my standards. The quietness of her three brothers and one sister made me think they did not like me. Oh well, for the time being I was impressed with Doris and her way of life.

Chapter 23

A Lifetime Commitment

In early January 1972, while Quentin and I were visiting our new companions, Doris got a phone call. Some fellow related to one of her students was calling her for a date. And what was worse, she accepted his offer. I was just a little miffed. After some time passed, I said, "Doris let's go for a ride." We went out west of Park View to a small park that was there at the time.

I do not remember much of what was said that night, except it ended up with my asking Doris to marry me. Her response did not come quickly. She obviously was not expecting such a request. After what seemed like ten minutes, she told me she would marry me. The smile on my face, and the smile on Doris's face, were fixed for the rest of the evening. We went back to our apartments and made our announcement to Eta and Quentin.

That same night after I returned home, I got down on my knees beside my bed and thanked God for this miracle in my life. At the same time I asked Jesus to take charge of my life. I believed what Jesus said in John 3:16, "For God so loved the world, that He gave His only begotten Son, that whoever believes in Him should not perish, but have eternal life." This was the same Jesus that Doris and Eta had been encouraging me to get to know.

I now believed what I had been reading in John: Jesus was crucified, buried, and that He rose again three days later. The small-child faith I learned in Highland Methodist Church, was now the faith of an adult, who knew it to be true. Oh, I did not, and still do not understand everything, but I knew enough to keep pursuing Jesus.

In the next six months, Doris and I prepared for a June 24th wedding. We bought a house on 4611 Harrison in Davenport. We bought various items of furniture during the spring. I moved in after the house closing in May. There was fear and trembling in our hearts as we signed a 30-year mortgage. We did not know what was ahead, but we signed those long-term papers, just as our parents, and grandparents had signed their mortgages and marriage licenses before us.

On our wedding day, my parents and their entourage ate way too long at a restaurant in Davenport. When they realized they were cutting it close they raced all the way to the Clinton Church of Christ. They were very close to walking in with the bride. Mom would break out in a sweat every time that story was told. They had Marvin, who was standing up with me, and Angela, a flower girl, riding with them. There is a rumor there was some speeding that day along Highway 67, the river road.

Doris and I honeymooned in the Wisconsin Dells. We stopped in Chicago to take in a Cubs doubleheader. We might have seen it all, if I had not gotten off the interstate way too early in downtown Chicago. We did not spend real long on our honeymoon, as we were both looking forward to Doris moving into our new house. For better or worse we were committed.

Wedding Picture

Wedding Picture with Parents

Left to right - Leonard and Velma Jess, Doris and
Keith, Norma Jean and Arden Wood

Chapter 24

Bettendorf Christian Church (BCC)

Bettendorf Christian Church has been our church home for 46 years. I was immersed here, in Christian baptism, back in the spring of 1972 after I committed my life to Jesus. Karl Roberts, the minister, did the honors. Karl has been a mentor for me over the years.

Karl included Doris and me in the young couples' Bible study group called 'Serendipity'. He got me playing for the softball team. He took me calling on potential church members with him. He encouraged me to attend Bible College with the thought of possibly becoming a full-time minister.

Doris and I later decided that full-time ministry was not for us, after a summer of youth ministry at BCC. We moved back to Bettendorf and I took up teaching math again in the Davenport School System. Within a year of returning from Bible College, I was voted in as an elder of BCC, a position I held off and on for over 22 years.

Our best friends during this period came from the couples represented on this leadership team: Karl and Sharon Roberts, Lowell and Carol Haan, Don and Sandy Paustian, and Mike and Ruth Senneff. All these couples, except Karl and Sharon, have moved to other cities and churches for various reasons. Time and aging has a way of moving us around.

There were lots of leadership activities we participated in on a monthly basis. I am going to skip the long meetings and tough decisions we had to make over the years. Instead I want to tell you about the funniest things this group did together. We regularly put on skits at various church functions. Don and Lowell could do the funniest skit with Don being a prize fighter, Rocky, who probably would lose to his shadow.

The all time best for me, was our presentation of the dating game. We men, dressed up as women, going out of our way to look ridiculous. The fun started as we were dressing up in the men's bathroom. Various restaurant patrons came into a crowded bathroom where four men were making themselves look like ladies.

We men were having a good time watching each other get ready in our fashion-less dresses. The audience was approximately 100 'Sweetheart Banquet' church attenders. When we made our grand entrance, Don started kissing men on the forehead leaving a big lipstick imprint. Lowell paraded around with his tall skinny legs blowing kisses to the crowd. Mike was a real beauty with his mustache and a big smile. It is a fond memory of the many fun times we had together.

BCC always worked to get people into small groups. According to church statistics, people will move on to another church if they do not have some relatively close friends within six months. Doris and I have been in a lot of different small groups over the years. Some as leaders and some as participants. We were high school youth sponsors with the Coxs and the Hills in the mid-80's. I have participated in several men's accountability groups and family Bible studies in homes. The small groups I currently participate in are my Sunday school class, our Plus-50 social group, and a men's accountability group with Steve Thomsen, Scott Allen, and Merrill Davis.

Karl and Sharon always liked picnics and potlucks. I am glad they did. They would always have an all-church Memorial Day picnic at Scott County Park. There was always a large crowd, a big softball game, and way more good food than we could eat.

It would be a mistake to infer that life at BCC has always been wonderful. Like any family, we have had our ups and downs. Being on the leadership team especially brings disagreements and even hard feelings at times. There have been times I considered going to another church, but the draw of close friendships always pulled me back.

Our boys had many close friends at BCC. They were a part of lots of Sunday school classes, church camps, youth groups, and Christmas programs. We owe a lot of our family's spiritual growth to the preaching, teaching, and encouragement we have received at BCC.

At my current stage in life, it becomes harder to replace old friends. Some of the closest have passed away. If we moved to a new city, or a new church, it would take a while to form a new, close knit Sunday school class. I think we will stay here, where our friends are, the friends that have supported us over the years, and who believe in the same Savior we do.

Chapter 25

New Adventure — Bible College

It was 6 years after graduation from UNI, and 2 years after getting married. I was growing in my new found faith. North Scott was a good school system, but I felt challenged to try a new occupation. I decided I would like to be a minister, or at least study in that direction. We had saved some money with two teacher salaries for two years.

We packed our bags and moved, from Davenport to Iowa Christian College in Des Moines, Iowa. It was a new college in an old facility that needed lots of work to become an attractive learning environment. We went there thinking I could get a Bible College education, and help this new college get started. There was a lot to do. I kept busy taking classes and working on improving the property.

Doris got a job teaching Jr. High Math in the Norwalk School System. In the second half of the school year our first son, Marcus, was born. It was an exciting time for us. I can remember thinking, I hope Doris knows how to handle a new baby, because I had no insight to share.

The school year went well, but we realized the educational opportunities were limited in this new college. We decided to transfer to Lincoln Christian College in Lincoln, Illinois. This was a well established college with more teachers with lots of experience. I learned a lot about the Bible and its teachings.

Doris and I slowly, over the school year, decided that we were not really cut out to be a full-time ministry family. We further cemented this decision by working as a youth minister that summer at BCC. After the hectic summer we were ready to go back to teaching.

I filled out a job application to teach in the Davenport school system. I got an interview and a job offer to teach at Smart Jr. High as a 9th grade math teacher and coach. We moved again, quickly as the new school year was close to starting. We purchased a house at 1855 Queens Drive in Bettendorf.

One picture that sticks in my mind from the three moves was looking in the rear view mirror of a big U-haul to see Doris in our car right behind me. She was not a fan of moving, but there she was through it all.

Chapter 26

Back to Teaching — Frank L Smart

Back to teaching, but I was the one about to get the education. This school was named after Frank L. Smart, a Harvard graduate who became the superintendent of the Davenport School system from 1907-1936. This Jr. High was in western Davenport, in the inner city. A high percentage of the students were poor Hispanics.

I just read on my smart phone, while writing this, that today Frank L Smart Junior High ranks worse than 99.4% of middle schools in Iowa. It also ranked last among the five ranked middle schools in Davenport.

I was to teach 9th grade Geometry, Algebra and General Math. This assignment was a real culture shock for a farm boy. There were several mornings when I just wanted to keep going west on Locust rather than turning down the Fejevary Park hill to Smart.

Once I toughened up, I realized that the Geometry and Algebra students were good kids. The two sections of General Math were what made the job challenging. A good share of these 9th grade General Math students had given up, and had no real desire to learn or even be in school.

I am talking the late 1970's. I'm sure teachers today would say things were easier back then. But in my mind, this was a tough teaching assignment.

My other assignment at Smart was to coach 9th grade wrestling. At North Scott, I had so many boys wrestling I could not give them all proper attention. At Smart, I had to recruit a couple wrestlers just to fill out the lineup. I had a wrestling team of 12 boys. I had some good wrestlers, but no 9th grade boys wanted to waste their time being a second team wrestler. It was a real challenge getting all of the 12 guys to practice.

In my final year at Smart we had a pretty good team that could compete with any 9th grade team in the area. We were wrestling some good matches. In fact we ended with an 8-3 record, and came close to winning the city tournament. At one meet, one of my heaviest guys, a young tough guy I had recruited out of the halls, was getting man handled by a very good wrestler from Pleasant Valley. After the referee raised the PV wrestler's arm in victory, my guy hauled off and slugged him.

If that wasn't embarrassing enough, my guy took off running out of the gym, like it was a street fight. Fortunately for me, my principal was there to corral the runaway. That experience happened very near the time I applied to be a government accountant.

Chapter 27

Being a Family Man

I have been putting this chapter off. Doris is proofreading everything I write. She corrects my punctuation and grammar. She changes my bad choices, like when to use there or their. Probably, every chapter I make a mistake in the use of where or were. Between us, we are making our way through these memoirs.

In this chapter, I am pretty confident she will say, "That isn't the way I remember it", or "How can you say that?" But it is time to assert myself and tell it as I see it. First of all I have to thank Doris for being very supportive through this new writing adventure.

As far as being a family man, I would say I have been a better father than husband. I always enjoyed doing things with the boys, the same things I enjoyed doing when I was young. I like to go to parks. I like riding my bicycle in the early morning. I like playing catch and kicking balls. I enjoy the competition of games. I still enjoy coloring and drawing, especially when I have a young boy next to me at church.

We were and are a family who does things together. Together often meant the boys on teams, and mom and dad watching or coaching. Together meant going to church activities every

Sunday. I was in charge of having a devotion time each night, and rehashing their daily activities at bedtime.

I like to hear my boys analyzing sports of all kinds, especially soccer. I thought I knew a lot about soccer. I had read books, and watched educational tapes. When the boys got older, and had experienced playing, they saw things and explained strategy that was beyond me.

It was a sad time for me, as the boys got older and went to college. As they graduated, there was not one thing I could do to help the boys in their chosen professions. In earlier times, on the farm, farmers learned to do a little of everything. They had no choice. If something broke down on the farm you fixed it with baling wire, or duct tape, or whatever else was needed. You could not afford to buy new, or bring in a professional.

Being a jack-of-all-trades and a master of none fits my mentality. The boys specialize in what they do (soccer coaching, engineering, and being a lawyer). They look up any unknowns on YouTube to see if they can solve the problem. If they can not solve the issue they hire a professional to do whatever is needed.

Doris and I have been a good team working with the boys. I think I cried more than she did as each one left home. I was responsible to make sure the boys obeyed their mother. From my husband standpoint, I left a lot of the unpleasant work to her. I did not change many diapers. Doris was the one who got up in the middle of the night. Doris attended the teacher conferences and took the boys to the doctor. I am not proud of what I did, it just happened that way. Did I mention I was a selfish person?

Doris is and always has been a hard worker. If I did not do something, or did something poorly she corrected it quietly. I did most of the outside work, and she did the inside work. We were often most comfortable when working separately, doing our own thing. She has long since decided that I was no help when she went shopping. Every so often, I would try to help her with inside work. I usually came away deciding I was better off staying outside.

Doris and I are both conflict avoidance people. We would rather do more work ourselves than take a chance at irritation. So when we have our occasional disagreements, there is a silence around our house. These quiet times have decreased, and they are over much quicker than they used to be.

There are family issues we have just left alone for the most part. Doris's family is rather quiet. I thought they really disliked me the first time I went to her home. My family is loud and proud of it. Back on the farm, the Wood family had company in without even thinking about it. Doris isn't comfortable with company until the whole house is clean.

Doris likes to have the TV on. I would prefer to listen to the radio. Doris likes Hallmark movies. I like Rambo and documentaries on Hitler. We have compromised more lately, watching the daily news and Cubs games. Less and less do we watch TV in separate rooms. We now realize our preferences are neither right or wrong, they just are. More recently, we have started turning off the TV, with both of us reading a good book.

We have learned we are two, sometimes selfish, independent people who decided to get married and share life together.

Separation or divorce were never an option for us. Our marriage was based on a lifetime commitment to each other, and to the great God we serve. Doris and I have been and are good for each other.

As we age our marriage is still improving. I think we are both enjoying the fact, that we have mellowed over the years. Our roles are now well defined. Being in control is not the issue it once was. We enjoy being together more than we ever have. The largest share of our travel is to see family. I do not see that trend changing any time soon.

Around the Table

Sitting (left to right) - Marc, Doris, and Keith
Standing (left to right) - David and Dan

Chapter 28

Government Accounting — RIA

I have to admit, I did not choose the profession that went with my natural desires and abilities. I really enjoyed coaching any sport. Next I enjoyed teaching (especially Algebra and Sunday school), and coming in third was Accounting. Not that I disliked accounting, I just never dug into it with enthusiasm. I wanted someone to train me, as opposed to my learning on my own.

I moved to the Rock Island Arsenal (RIA) in January of 1980, leaving Jr. High math and a coaching position at Frank L. Smart. I was now 34 years old. My decision was based on two things. I wanted to make more money per year, and I wanted to have a bigger retirement nest egg at the end of my career. Doris was staying home with the boys while they were young. We both felt that was the best thing for all of us.

I was able to coach our boys in their sports, baseball and soccer. I was able to teach Sunday school class each Sunday, so my first two loves would be met in different ways.

When I retired in 2006 from the Arsenal, I had earned more money per year than I would have as a teacher. My retirement savings was considerably more than it would have been had I retired as a teacher.

So did I make a good decision? Who knows. Like many other decisions in life you decide, and then you live with the decision. Doris and I have been able to live comfortably, and do all the things we wanted to do. She was able to stay home with the boys in their younger years. She retired as a 1st and 2nd grade teacher at Bettendorf Community School District in 2011.

As far as my work in accounting, my position changed at least six times over the years. I was always a little behind the new accounting methods and new accounting systems. I liked using an adding machine, recording my work in journals and ledgers, and using a sharp number 2 lead pencil.

Being the insightful person I was, I predicted early that the computer would never be able to replace the good old pencil and paper. Forget that. Every new office I moved to had their own systems that required more passwords. Other offices that worked with us had their own systems we were expected to learn and use. As the use of computers kept increasing, I felt, I was just hanging on. By the time I retired, my job had completely passed me by. It probably wasn't as bad as I made it sound, but I was never called back in for my expertise after I retired.

There were a lot of good people I worked with over the years. I missed them and the humor we shared in the office. I tried very hard to do things that made people laugh. Harmony in the office was important to me. The work itself I never missed.

I can guarantee you I do not miss crossing the Mississippi River on the I-74 bridge, especially on cold winter days. I did not miss trying to find a parking spot somewhere near the office. We had flex-time so we could pretty much start when you wanted within reason. I usually started work at 6:15 in the morning so that I could get off at 2:45 in the afternoon. The traffic was lighter at those times.

Now, in retirement, I enjoy keeping busy doing things that challenge but do not overwhelm. I finished our basement the year after I retired. I have had one or two part-time jobs most of the years I have been retired. We visit each of the boys in their homes at least once a year. I have learned to enjoy books ranging from historic novels, financial investing, retirement, self-improvement, and Christian living. I love to garden and get my hands in the dirt. I would love to have a good reason to own a medium size tractor to mow and till the soil. However, age is dictating that my next move will be to downsize rather than to take up farming.

Chapter 29

Slow-Pitch Softball

I had forgotten how much fun it was playing ball with the guys. I was sold on my new faith in Jesus and our new church, Bettendorf Christian Church (BCC). But then I was asked if I would like to play softball with the church softball team. Are you kidding? Would I like a piece of cherry pie with ice cream on it? Of course I would be willing to join the team.

Almost immediately I had a whole group of new friends. Friends who liked playing ball, giving each other a bad time, and just being together. I started out playing third base but over the years I played about every infield position.

One of my early, self-centered discoveries was that every team puts their weakest player in right field. (My apologies to all the great right fielders out there.) In no time at all I learned to place the ball consistently into right field. With my competitive spirit, I just wanted to be on base and score runs.

I had my own way to evaluate our teams. If I was catching, we were pretty darn good. If I was playing third base we were pretty average. If I was playing shortstop, we were in trouble.

Lowell Haan was our ace slow-pitch pitcher. He has a good sense of humor. He needed it. He got pelted more than once by throws down to second base. The funniest play I ever saw started with a big swing and a ball dribbling out in front of the home plate. Our catcher pounced on that ball like a cat. He fired the ball to second base to nail the advancing runner. Lowell hit the deck to keep from getting beaned. The throw was so strong it went up the alley between our two unsuspecting outfielders. The ball got back to the cut-off man as the hitter crossed the plate, for a two run homer.

Lowell, one of my best friends even today, and his wife moved to Decatur, Illinois to be near their youngest daughter's family. I inherited his pitching position. I really enjoyed the opportunity, and found out I could throw strikes fairly consistently. Being one to keep my own statistics, secretly of course, I was the winning pitcher in almost 100 games.

May I brag just a little more. One year, in the second half of my career, I had a batting average of .633, and a .750 on-base-percentage. The right fielders must have been exceptionally weak that year. I hit 6 home runs in my slow-pitch career. Each time the balls I hit were hooking and spinning into right field close to the foul line. The hits then went into foul territory with no out-of-bounds line. I don't think I ever hit a ball over an outfielder's head. One team put a shift on to get me out. I was not to be outdone. I hit a double down the third base line.

I played on the BCC team for more than 20 years, retiring at age 48. One of the saddest moments of my life was hanging up my BCC team jersey for the last time. As a hitter, I was having trouble hitting the ball past the second basemen. At the same time, I realized I couldn't throw strikes as consistently as I wanted to.

One very patient team had a lot of guys who were willing to take walks. I could not make them pay for that decision. One added dilemma was those new aluminum bats. Some big hitters sent their hits over the mound like a shot. I found myself being scared when they came to bat.

We usually played games on minimally maintained ball fields. Who cared, it was all for fun. One weekend we had a big church tournament on our home diamond. I spent a good share of the day preparing the field by mowing grass and chalking the infield to look like Wrigley Field. That may be a little bit of an exaggeration.

It just so happened that I was the lead off hitter when our team came to bat. On the first pitch of my at bat, I hit a nice liner to right field. I was immediately called out by the volunteer umpire for stepping outside of the batter's box. As you can tell, I am still a little bitter. This was the first time we had had a batter's box all year, and I was the one who spent the day preparing it.

I truly enjoyed playing slow-pitch softball. It was the one time, as I aged, I could still think of myself as an athlete.

I need to thank Doris for letting me play all those slow pitch games for 20 years. I don't know that I ever missed a game.

Thanks also to my teammates, (Lowell, Karl, Don, Jack, Denny, Louie, Kenny, Gary, Jim, Chuck, Ron, Billie, Brad, Kirk, Del, Blair, Steve, Tony, Doug, Roger, and Dennis) for all the fun we had together. My apologies to the many other comrades, whose names I left off this list. I don't remember names like I used to. I have even forgotten the name of that umpire who called me out for stepping outside the batter's box.

Chapter 30

Becoming the Soccer Family

Warning. If you thought I was too braggadocios before, you may want to skip this chapter. Doris and I have three wonderful boys. They are not wonderful all the time, but often enough, that we round up to 'wonderful'.

With my love of baseball, I had these three out hitting and playing catch more than they wanted to be. We lived right across the street from Kiwanis Park. The park was great for baseball practice. When no one was playing tennis, the tennis courts made a handy practice field. As they got a little older, I coached several of their baseball teams. We always did well. We were a competitive bunch.

In about 1988, when Marc was 13, Dan was 10, and David was 7, they came to me and said, "You know, Dad, if we had our choice, we like soccer a whole lot more than baseball. Baseball is too boring. There is way too much standing around." After I recovered from this foolish talk, we became a soccer family.

Marc was the initiator of the soccer push. He loved the game. He dribbled the ball everywhere he went. He juggled the ball by the hour. Amazingly, the younger two boys followed his leading, and worked on their skills. They worked their way up from park board soccer onto traveling soccer teams. All of them had decent speed, and handled the ball well with their feet.

I simply must tell you about my Dad visiting, when the boys were younger. Dad said why don't you and I show these boys how to play keep away. Dad had never played soccer in his life. He just assumed two adults could handle three young boys. Honest truth is that Dad and I never completed one pass. The boys loved showing off.

As time passed, all five of us, including Doris, really enjoyed watching and/or playing soccer. We went at least monthly to a soccer tournament somewhere. We stayed in motels and dorms as a family. We would seek out a church on Sunday mornings. There were at least four times when we led a church service, in a park or at a large motel meeting room, inviting other families to join us. We learned quickly it was easier to ask forgiveness for using a room than getting the proper permission.

For the next ten years, our family traveled all over the Iowa and Illinois area, going to soccer tournaments. I rarely recommend this plan of action to other families, but it worked well for us. I got busy reading and learning soccer so I could coach it. I did end up coaching several of their youth teams.

I thoroughly enjoyed coaching soccer to young boys in the 8-14 age range. They were so full of enthusiasm for the game. Much of my coaching involved learning while playing. I really enjoyed playing the game myself. The plan worked well until these young men and their parents knew as much about soccer as I did.

Dave Codling and Mike Beck, fellow coaches, spent an inordinate amount of time learning the game with me. We became good friends while teaching our boys what we could of soccer. There were so many players, parents, and coaches that made this a special time for me and our family.

Within their playing years, all three boys got to experience winning an Iowa state soccer championship. Doris was very happy when all the various sized trophies were gone. What a pain they were to dust. All three boys are among the top six or seven leading goal scorers in Bettendorf High School history. David was chosen Gatorade Iowa High School player of the year in 1998-1999.

All three played soccer all four years in college and became captains of their teams. The older two boys played at Olivet Nazarene in Kankakee, IL., with David playing for Wheaton College in Wheaton, IL. Both colleges were close enough that Doris and I could watch several of their games.

Marc (age 43), has been the head women's soccer coach at Hardin-Simmons University (HSU) for 17 years now. HSU is a Division III college with approximately 2,000 students. In 2010, he coached his team to the National Championship. I have to say that was one of the thrills of my life, watching his team win eight big games in a row, knocking off the 3-time reigning champion for the title. Marc was subsequently named the NCAA coach of the year for DIII.

The final two games of the national tournament were played in San Antonio, Texas the home of Ft. Sam Houston. I toured the Army grounds that had been my training base in 1969. Almost everything had changed in the intervening 40 years. The old Brook Army Hospital had been abandoned, and given way to a new high rise hospital.

Marc has always shared information about his team with me, such as team lineups, how he thinks his team can win a certain game, and new recruits that have committed to Hardin-Simmons. I am quite sure I know more of his team's statistical history than any other fan. Marc has allowed me to attend pregame meetings and half-time talks. A couple times he allowed me to lead the team in prayer after their games. As I have always loved coaching, just being included in his work has been this father's dream.

The other two boys did some assistant soccer coaching after college, but decided on other professions. Dan is now an engineer for the Daimler Group near Charlotte, North Carolina. David is a lawyer in the public defender's office, in Medford, Oregon. All three boys are married and have a boy and a girl. I am not sure any of their children will be soccer players, but that's fine. What concerns me is who is going to love and care for those baseball gloves in my dresser drawer.

The boys ran Woody's Soccer Club for many years

Left to right - Daniel, Marcus, David, and Arden (Grandpa Wood)

Chapter 31

Sunday School

This may seem like an unusual topic for a memoir. Teaching an adult Sunday school class has been the natural way for me to share my faith. I enjoy learning and teaching what I have learned. I wanted to share Jesus with others. I wanted to share what I had learned in Bible College. This class has been a 40-year labor of love.

There is a push in many churches today to get every one in a small group of fellow believers. This class has been that small group for me. We are an unlikely group of friends held together by our belief that the Bible is God's word. We believe the gospel message: that Jesus was crucified, that He was buried, and that He rose from the grave three days later.

As a class we have studied many books of the Bible, with an emphasis on the New Testament, and further emphasis on the life of Jesus and His church. In 2018, we have been watching CD's put out by Focus on the Family, narrated by Ray Vander Laan, related to the land of Israel. I would highly recommend any of his 15 CDs, if you are looking for relevant Sunday school material.

If any of you readers are ever in the Bettendorf area on Sunday morning at 9:00, we would love to have you join us. We can always add more chairs to our circle of approximately 20 people.

Please allow me to recognize some people who have been my close friends and fellow learners over the years.

<u>Past members</u> who were so faithful, but have moved on – Clarence and Jewell Whitrock, Earl and Pat Johnson, Ron and Miriam Neeson, Ron and Gale George, Ray Boston, Stephanie Ferguson, Tim Stringham, Pam O'Briant, Ann Worthington, Rich Dvorak, and Joyce Mcnamara. My apologies for those who were part of the class and feel like they should have been included here. You should have been. Again my apologies.

<u>Current members</u> who attend regularly include Les and Joyce Weinkauf, Tom and Jan Amyette, Mike and Audrey Birmingham, Vic and Pam Crome, Sandee Clark, Jerry and Teresa Clark, Merrill and Carol Davis, Henry and Pia Ammann, Leora Blackwood, Mary Brunner, Faith Timm, Dennis Anhalt, Jerry and Yuvonne Yowell, Arnie and Sandy Ziebarth, Keith Theus, and Dean Havill.

Chapter 32

White Elephant Gift Exchange

How could I wait so long to share our 'White Elephant Gift Exchange'? About 10 years ago, Mom and Dad were telling their family to quit buying them Christmas gifts. They had everything they wanted. Their gift, according to them, was just having the family together. They had been saying that for quite some time, to no avail.

After some discussion, it was decided we should have a white elephant gift exchange. Why not have some fun with the gift giving time? Rules included, you could not spend more than a dollar on a gift - think garage sales. Gifts could be used items from your closet, attic, or garage. They did not even have to be functional. A hedge trimmer with a cut electrical cord would be perfect. Used underwear was ruled out.

Larry's gift of half a box of chocolates, with many of the remaining chocolates half eaten, may have gotten the biggest laugh. His wife, Judy, brought the traveling, beat-up suitcase that contained a loud blue sports jacket and matching tie. Each year the proud winner gets to add another clothing item.

Oh, there have been some detractors from this gala event. Some will not bring gifts for fear of what they might have to take home. Hosts of the yearly gathering make a rule all gifts have to be removed from the premises. The sewer pipe gift, and the car tune-up leftovers gift, may have been a big factor there. It is rumored some gifts end up in the first rest area dumpster on the way home. Surely not.

Each year more and more kids get involved. It is like a used items treasure hunt. It is grand watching parents tell their kids, "No don't take that." One other strategy is to take the smallest gift as it will be easy to take to its new home. Gifts can be stolen, if you see a previously opened gift you want. Some have stolen small, clean gifts to avoid a bigger gift, still wrapped in a Hy-Vee bag. The formal gift wrap is last week's comic pages.

Every one has a comment of some kind as the gift exchange begins. Some groan and make derogatory remarks. Others are fighting for front row seats. Many times there are more gifts than people wanting to claim them. Some lucky persons will get two gifts.

It is just fun to watch the looks on people's faces. Mom and Dad loved it before they passed away. Dad told me to bring a gift for him when he was living in a nursing home. The groans, the harassment, the joking, the laughter make the white elephant gift exchange one of the few events that can take precedence over the Wood card game.

Chapter 33

Caring for Others

In June of 1990, Duck Creek, which goes right through Bettendorf, flooded. It caused a lot of damage ruining several houses in low lying areas. Some basements caved in. Some were full of mud. I knew some people who lived in those homes. I chose not to get involved. I guess I embarrassed myself at my lack of caring. Our house was up high, so we had no problem.

Since that time, I've changed my ways and have gotten involved locally. I also have gone on several mission trips. I have found them to be some of the most rewarding times of my life. I prefer U.S. trips because there is no language barrier, no translators. I also do better at short-term trips. When trips get to be two weeks or longer, I am ready to be home.

The following are the places I have been privileged to work:

Mexico: This was my first mission trip. We paid for, and built a house, about the size of a double-car garage, for a needy family. We had way too many people for the amount of work being done. My youngest son, David, who could speak some Spanish, went with me. This trip was a little frustrating as we probably could have built two of these structures if we would have had the materials.

<u>Haiti:</u> If Mexico was Missions 101, Haiti was a graduate class. We were in Haiti a little over two weeks in 2002. This is the poorest nation in the world. I was able to clean teeth during much of the stay, using my Army training. We had people lined up for cleaning most of the day. I started to notice that some of the later people had clean teeth. What was happening was, they were coming back for a second cleaning. They wanted a second sample tube of toothpaste and the toothbrush we were giving each patient as they left. Other members of our team shared Jesus, or preached as the opportunities arose. One morning, a disabled child was found just inside our compound crying. Her parents had given her up to the mission, thinking the child would have a better chance at life with the missionaries.

<u>Ukraine:</u> This was a two week trip in 2004 to help with the construction of Tavriski Christian Institute (TCI) a new Bible College in Kherson, Ukraine. I stepped on a nail and had to get a tetanus shot in a Ukrainian health facility. The construction work was limited due to the lack of funds for building materials. The second week we provided a vacation Bible school for the community of Chaplinka, Ukraine.

<u>Hurricane Katrina:</u> This was one of the most costly hurricanes ever, hitting in August of 2005. The lower part of the city of New Orleans became inundated with water. We went as a team of 16 to gut houses. We averaged a house a day. We were there for a week. They really wanted us to stay longer and come back. They said the teams from Iowa really knew how to work, and with no supervision. It doesn't take a lot of training to gut houses and take the debris to the curb. Our first trip was four months after the hurricane. We went again four months later.

What an experience. Dan, our middle son, was able to join us for the second trip.

Campus House, Univ of Missouri: The Christian Campus House in Columbia, Missouri, purchased a very run down, but structurally sound fraternity house. A team from BCC helped them build rooms to house college students in 2006. We went three times that first year. We have been going back each June since, for one-week work trips. We do work projects they are not able to get to during the school year. The director, Lance Tamerius, does a tremendous job working with 100+ student residents. All residents get cheaper rent in the Campus House, but they are all required to attend Bible studies and be involved with at least one Christian ministry during the year.

Honduras: This was a two-week trip with a medical emphasis in 2007. Once again I was able to clean teeth for the whole time. This was one of those countries where you leave the driving to the professionals. The biggest truck has the right-of-way. Also a loud horn comes in handy. Police carry military weapons openly. One morning, a young man was shot and killed waiting on a bus. The volunteers who saw it were pretty shaken. While I cleaned teeth, other team members shared the gospel message with all the people who came for medical treatment.

Deaf Missions, Council Bluffs, Iowa: In 2011 and 2013 we went to Deaf Missions to do some maintenance jobs they had not been able to do in their daily routine. We painted the exterior of their main building. I was up on a scaffolding three stories up, which is way beyond my comfort level. We cleaned carpets and spruced up the grounds around the building. Each time we were able to help them get out their quarterly mailing.

EF5 Tornado that hit Joplin: This tornado hit in May of 2011. The destruction was overwhelming. On this particular trip I went two weeks with the Red Cross. I was allowed to run a shelter that housed many of the Red Cross workers in a junior high gym. The work I did was something that needed to be done. I personally would have rather been out in the ruins working with a chainsaw.

Ukraine: This 2017 trip was also over two-weeks long. In the Ukraine, public schools will allow Christian groups to come in and put on what we would call 'Vacation Bible School'. We had three inflatable bounce houses as attractions for young people. We had two or three teams going out daily. Each team went to three schools or churches each day. I was allowed to preach a couple times on the weekends during this trip. Preaching is different speaking through an interpreter. One day we had a group of Muslim children come. Their parents allowed them to participate if they stayed outside the Christian church. Who knows how many lives we affected during those two weeks? It was quite an experience.

I did not list these to brag about what I have done. As I hinted at earlier, I am the beneficiary of the joy of working, and helping others. My hope is, that I can encourage others to step out of their comfort zone, and help where needed. There are so many ministries available, both far away or right in your own back yard.

Chapter 34

Two Very Special Trips

I have had the opportunity to take several trips. I enjoy traveling, so I appreciate the opportunities. By our sons living so far away from Iowa, we have at least one annual trip to see each of them. Likewise, mission trips have taken me to corners of the world I would never have seen otherwise. But this chapter is about the two trips that were very special to me as a tourist.

The first trip was to Israel and Jerusalem in October of 2011. Some Young at Heart members came up with the plan. Karl and Sharon Roberts became the organizers of the trip. It ended up being an eleven day trip with stops in Tel Aviv, Ceasarea Philippi, Capernaum, Nazareth, Jericho, Bethlehem, Masada, and finally Jerusalem. What a thrill it was to walk where Jesus himself, walked and taught.

Many of the actual sites mentioned in the Bible have a church of some faith erected over it. Tourism is alive and well in Israel. The place where the Sermon on the Mount was given, is a big complex, with tour buses jostling for position. The same is true of the place where Jesus was baptized in the Jordan River. Tourists and entrepreneurs really have no way of knowing the exact spot of the baptism. Some of us including myself, were baptized in the Jordan River.

A few places like the Sea of Galilee, the Jordan River, and the Dead Sea, are natural features that may be very close to what Jesus saw. We got to boat across the Sea of Galilee in the early morning. We saw shepherds on the barren hills. We took a tram to the top of Masada. Masada really tested my fear of heights.

We got to walk the same streets that Jesus walked in Jerusalem. We had a communion service in the Garden of Gethsemane. We went inside the empty tomb. It would have been nice to sit and meditate, but many more people were in line behind us. We went right up to the Wailing Wall, and viewed what remains of the temple. What a thrill. I am ready to go again if the opportunity arises.

The second trip was a tour of many of the World War I and World War II sites in Europe. I am still thanking Mike Senneff and the four Steenlage brothers, for allowing my brother Marvin and me to join them on the 14 day adventure, in June of 2014.

I had read quite a little about D-Day and WWII and the Holocaust, but to go and stand where these historic events took place was quite an experience. We walked on Omaha and Utah beaches, in northern France, where the American troops landed on D-Day, June 6, 1944.

The trip was during the commemoration of the 70th anniversary of D-Day. Thirty-eight world leaders were gathered for this grand event, including President Obama and President Putin. Because all these dignitaries were present, we common tourists were not allowed in the D-Day landing area until later.

We traveled through the countries of Luxemburg, France, Germany, Austria, Poland, the Czech Republic, and Belgium. We visited war sites at Verdun, the Somme Valley, Normandy, Bastogne, and the Eagles Nest, just to mention a few. We spent time in the cities of Paris, Salzburg, Krakow, Prague, Dresden, Frankfurt, and Nuremberg.

Early in the trip we visited the small city of Verdun and the Douaumont Ossuary. This as much as any other place pointed out the realities of war. The ossuary, a war monument, contained 130,000 skeletal remains of both French and German soldiers. From small ground level windows on the sides of the ossuary you could view the skeletal remains of thousands of unidentified men who died in the battles near Verdun.

This was the largest and longest battle of the First World War. Pounded by millions of artilliary rounds the battlefield became a featureless plain of churned mud and broken bodies. Supposedly the German plans called for two million artilliary rounds to be fired at French defenders in the first six days of this 10-month battle. Nine French villages were destroyed and never rebuilt. I did not realize that waring nations had that much fire power available in 1915.

The cost to both sides was 700,000 casualties (died, wounded, and missing). The total deaths were approximately 230,000. Wikipedia is a good source if you want to read more about the Battle of Verdun. After ten months of shelling and carnage on both sides, the French forces had recovered all the land lost earlier. Near the ossuary is one of the few places where the original battlefield has not been regraded back to farmland.

Walking there was like walking on an a large upside down egg carton.

Marvin and I climbed to the top of the 150 foot, artillery-shaped tower within the ossuary. Clear at the top the tower contains a bronze death-bell weighing two tons. The bell is sounded at official ceremonies and can be heard throughout the French countryside. It just so happened that Marvin and I were right next to the bell when it sounded. Boy did that death-bell rattle our teeth. We hurried down the many steps for fear they might sound the bell again.

Nine days later in our trip, our band of seven toured the Holocaust site at Auschwitz. Auschwitz was an army camp before it became the most notorious of all the Nazi concentration camps. Each brick building had a display of some aspect of the atrocities that went on there. We saw big masses of shaved hair, used shoes, old suit cases, used glasses, artificial limbs, kid's toys, baby clothes, and pictures of children that had been left behind as families marched to their deaths.

We were led to areas where German's experimented on Jewish bodies, prison confinement areas, selection areas, undressing areas, gas chambers (so-called showers), and crematoriums. We looked at one area where people were shot at close range by firing squads.

The other killing facility in the area was Birkenau. two miles away. Birkenau was where many Jewish people were taken directly from the trains to the gas chambers. The sign at the entrance reads, "Work sets you free." Within the facility were the older wooden barracks and group toilets that you often see in history books. Large numbers of Jews were housed in these barracks. Many were put on work details where they were worked to exhaustion and death. For we American tourists this was a quiet and reflective day to say the least. How could all of this happen in a civilized world?

The 14-day trip was both thought provoking, and unforgettable. It was amazing to be driven around by the fearless Steenlage boys who were somewhat familiar with European driving. Watching them maneuver in the Paris madness, the narrow city streets all over Europe, and the high-speed Autobahn was something to behold. I would not even attempt that trip if I had to drive on my own.

Thanks again Mike.

Chapter 35

Dad's Big Decision

There is a saying among farmers, "Buy a good farm and you buy it once, buy a bad farm and you pay for it the rest of your life." Grandpa Wood had really stepped out on the ledge during the depression, and bought 320 acres of good, flat land in the Panora -Yale area. He had a wife and seven children to provide for. In a few years the economy turned around. Things went well financially for the family.

Grandpa and Grandma Wood were well healed financially by the time they retired from farm work in 1950. His land was now worth much more than he had paid for it. Grandpa was 70 years old, confident, set in his ways. He had helped Clyde and Ralph get started on nice farms close by the original homestead. In fact, the three of them shared their farm equipment. Two of the daughters, Lucille and Doris, had married, and lived on farms within five miles of Grandpa's farm.

Dad was the one son left. He was farming Grandpa's land along with another man, a cousin, Verne Wallace. Verne and Dad got along well. It seemed like Dad was next in line for Grandpa's support and possibly the homestead.

But for some reason, as brother Carroll and I are going to speculate, it did not work out that way. Carroll and I were somewhere between the ages of 3 and 5 at the time of Dad's big decision. Carroll is a farmer now. He farms close to the land Mom and Dad farmed for many years.

This is our theory of what happened back in 1950. Grandpa owned the farm and was in control of the whole operation. May I mention again, he was set in his ways? Dad was the youngest son, being close to 10 years younger than Clyde and Ralph. Grandpa told Dad what he thought Dad should do. More than likely, Grandpa thought Dad should rent his farm with the intention of possibly owning some day. Grandpa would do less and less in retirement, but would still be around. No doubt Grandpa would check to see how things were going.

Dad was not one to be told what he should and should not do. The older boys loved Dad, but teased him regularly, throughout his growing years. Dad laughed at the time, but he was not always laughing on the inside. Dad did not feel he would ever be respected by his family, as an equal.

He and Grandpa Wood went round and round, with Grandpa pointing out that he had a real opportunity here. All Dad could see was many more years of being the youngest son, and the youngest brother. With some real hard feelings growing between Grandpa and Dad, Dad decided he would strike out on his own.

Dad had $5,000 saved up to buy a farm. The bankers in the Panora – Yale area kind of laughed at Dad as he came in with that amount of money to buy a farm. The land value had increased greatly since Grandpa had purchased the original farm.

Not to be put off in his decision to move, he looked at poorer land more in his price range. He and Mom found an 80 acre farm west of Fontanelle that could be purchased with the $5,000 and a loan of $6,000. This land had hills and rocks and more clay. It would be a lot of work, but Mom and Dad were not ones to back away from work.

Dad always spoke of himself as the 'black sheep' of the family. I believe this big decision was the main thing that prompted him to make that statement. Dad was a proud man. He would never admit that this decision might have been a mistake. He was not about to ask for help. He may have spent a good share of his lifetime trying to show his Dad, and the rest of his family, that he could be successful too.

Seeing what Grandpa went through in the depression left a strong impression on Dad and Mom. My folks always went with the least expensive, least risky purchase. They always felt the next depression might be just around the corner. They could not risk losing what they had.

Clyde offered to help them buy more land. Mom and Dad turned him down for fear they would be mortgaging the farm they owned. Any money they saved went right into certificates of deposit. They considered that money safe.

Dad was able to pay off all his debts and build a modest, new house with the money he inherited from Grandpa and Grandma Wood. Can you imagine the burden that must have been removed from Dad's back? And yet, there was the disappointment he felt that his now, relatively wealthy father, was giving him money.

Money he needed so badly. Dad was still struggling to make ends meet on his farm.

So these two men made their big decisions. Grandpa had become successful financially. Dad struggled financially most of his life. Oh, he would never have to worry about where they would stay and what they would eat. But compared to his Dad, he had no big estate to pass on at the end of his life.

His famous quote, to those who asked how they were doing was, "We are in good shape, for the shape we are in." I personally was surprised, in the final years of their lives, to find out just how tight their budget was.

As I study the depression, I notice that Grandpa was part of the prosperous 1920's before the depression. He had experienced good times and profited from them. He seemed to always be looking for the good times to return. He always bought better land. He was a chance taker and an opportunist. You have to admire his spirit. He was a hard man and a driver.

Dad's experiences from ages eight to eighteen were nothing but hard times. He never experienced real economic good times in his younger years. Dad worked just as hard as his father but always saw a depression ahead, rather than good times. His answer was to save what he had, rather than expand and grow. No doubt that was very logical considering what he and Mom had been through.

Dad and Grandpa forgave each other, for earlier hard feelings, before Grandpa died. They loved each other. I never heard Dad say anything derogatory about Grandpa. They both had families that loved them and would have done anything for them. And their God loved them.

They were both successful men in my eyes. They are both equals now, bowing at the feet of Jesus. I plan to join them, and you. (Romans 14:11) This fact prompted me to share this chapter.

Mom and Dad wanted their faith to be shared. That is why they spent several years at World Missionary Press in Indiana, printing gospel tracts for missionaries throughout the world. They returned to Des Moines to be near family and friends. Their home in Des Moines was still open to everyone, even after they were unable to come to the door and welcome visitors.

Chapter 36

Grieving the Losses

Mom passed away on April 13, 2015. She had been in hospice care for over two weeks. She visited with all who called as if there was no cancer to worry about. She had decided she did not want any more surgeries or extreme medications. She appeared so content. We prayed with her and read her scripture when she was no longer able to visit. One day I saw her reach toward heaven. By the next morning, she was gone.

The plan was for Dad to live in their house alone. We five boys had looked all over the area trying to find a senior facility that might work well for Dad. The best we could come up with was the nursing home in Mitchellville. It was nothing great, but the best we could find for what we needed. Our ultimate decision was for Dad to live in his own home. It would be lonely, but it was by far the most economical option.

The Thursday following the weekend funeral, I came from Bettendorf to visit Dad in his own home. It was a good day for Dad and me. We had several things to do, but no appointments and nothing that had to be done. We went to the Social Security office. We were there at 8:30 in the morning. I was third in line for the 9:00 office opening. At 8:55 Dad came balancing on his walker through the unorganized line of 25 people, just as we planned, so he would not have to stand so long.

When our number came up 10 minutes later, we found out Mom did not qualify for the $255 death benefit. Her 70 years as Dad's wife, working on the farm, at Missionary Press, as a carpenter and a mechanic aide was not enough. With no anger, we informed them there was no harder worker anywhere. We just wanted them to know. She had only worked four of the necessary 10 quarters required to qualify for the death benefit. They took a copy of Mom's death certificate.

As we traveled to the next item on the list, Dad told me the story of how Mom had nearly died giving birth to me. She was in the hospital three weeks recovering. Dad was busy running back and forth to the farm in Panora 50 miles away. He mentioned the thing that hurt him most was hearing his father-in-law say that he did not seem to care what happened to Norma Jean. This was the same father-in-law who did not come to their wedding.

By this time we were at Dad's bank where we presented them with Mom's death certificate. Within a matter of minutes, they changed their joint account to Dad's account alone. Dad got a hug from the lady he always worked with at the bank. All three times I had been with him, we sat and waited until she was done with someone else. Others asked if they could help us, but we had time. We would wait.

Next we were off to the post office to mail in Dad's insurance policy. We had decided to cash it out as it was an asset ($1,800) that needed to be liquidated. Dad directed where to turn at each corner. He wanted to go the way he would have taken if he had been driving. He went out of his way to stay off main roads and to cross at traffic lights.

Next we drove 10 miles to the State Farm office in Ankeny. We were going to cash in Mom's 70-year-old insurance policy. During hard times, they had taken out some of the cash value. The death benefit was $1,068. Dad was surprised it wasn't a little more than that. I could not argue with him on that.

By this time, it was time for lunch. Meals on Wheels arrived at his house right on time. Dad ate the pork chop meal. I ate the chili stew that had come the day before. At the meal, he said he had other errands he would like to run, if it was okay with me. We both were enjoying the time together. He would write his funeral thank you notes later, when he had no company.

So off we went to Menards in Altoona to get a grab-bar to put in front of Dad's stool. Dad rode around in an electric cart. There was no way he could walk those long aisles without assistance. But we were in no hurry. It was just a good day to be alive.

Next we went to the cheapest gas station in the area, according to Dad. He insisted on putting in $10 worth of gas, for all the driving around I had done. Our next stop was a Tobacco Outlet store. They had eggs on sale for 99 cents. Next stop was Hy-Vee for more groceries and a prescription.

But even before groceries, we had to get rid of three large boxes of pop cans and bottles. It must have been quite a sight seeing a 90-year-old man with his 69-year-old son jostling with all the other patrons, using the six can return machines. Even in all the confusion Dad was teaching me how to do it properly, in case my other sources of income went bad.

Inside Hy-Vee, I was to follow Dad around in his electric cart and assist as needed. As Dad was getting his prescription filled, I decided I would make my favorite ham, vegetables, and cheese omelets for Dad the next morning. I got the necessary ingredients to go with the 99 cent eggs. Mid-afternoon and we were ready to go home and install that grab-bar.

Dad was busy going back and forth to the garage for things, one of them being a heavy, old tool chest. He should have let me do the running, but you know how that is. He watched as I drilled holes, leveled, and tightened screws. In about 45 minutes, the job was done. We sat down for an afternoon break.

Throughout the day I heard about what a good wife Mom was. She stood by him no matter what he decided to do. He did not understand why Mom would never tell her boys how much she appreciated them. I heard several of Mom's opinions on things. Amazingly her opinions sounded a lot like Dad's opinions. They may have well been the same, I just never heard Mom express them.

After a half-hour break, I told Dad I had brought some flower starts from home, and I wanted to plant them in Mom's garden. I enjoyed digging in that wonderful black dirt. Dad was tired so he took a nap.

After supper, Larry Wiedemeyer and his wife came over for a nice visit. He was the one who always fixed Dad's snow blowers for him to resell. After they left, Dad and I both commented on what a nice day we had together. We both showered and went to bed.

Friday morning Dad was up by 6:30 shortly after I got up. I cooked him that omelet. I know it was nothing like what Mom fixed him every day for years. But his father taught him well. He cleaned up his whole plate.

After breakfast, we both realized my visit was coming to an end. He asked me if there was anything that Doris and I would especially like to have of theirs. I said I thought Mom wanted us to have the china that I sent her while I was in Viet Nam. Then I told Dad that it was more important to me, that we boys all remained close to each other, than I get any material things. What I really would like was a couple of buckets of Mom's black dirt for my garden. He had no problem with that.

I got my dirt as he looked on. Then I also claimed the shortest, most beat-up hoe that Mom had, so I could hoe with Mom's hoe. With tears in our eyes, we hugged each other and said goodbye. I drove out of view of the house, stopped the car, and I wept.

Chapter 37

Time Marches On

As time passes, so do the generations. Doris and I have been fortunate enough to raise three sons and have three lovely daughters-in-law. Each family has moved further away from Iowa than we would have liked.

Each family stays busier than they should, much like we did when were their age. They have built their own family traditions. It was our goal to have them be mature, productive members of society. It just wasn't supposed to happen so quickly. We did not intend that they would be quite this independent.

Marcus and Kelley (Tregesser) now live in Abilene, Texas where they have resided for over 17 years. Marc is the head women's soccer coach at Hardin-Simmons University. Kelley is currently working for junior achievement. She was a junior high school teacher for the two years before that. Her current job allows her more time with our grandchildren, Kamryn (10) and Alexander (6). They are all a pleasure to be around.

Dan and Mari (Kasamoto) now live near Charlotte, North Carolina. They recently moved from Murfreesboro, Tennessee. Before that, they lived several years in Honolulu, Hawaii, where Mari was born and raised. Dan just recently became an engineer with Daimler Group. Mari is an occupational therapist who is currently staying home with daughter Kolbe (4) and son Elikai (1). Doris and I are pleased she is able to do that. These precious children keep Mari busy.

David and Tanya (Skaletsky) now live in Medford, Oregon. David is a lawyer in the public defender's office. Tanya is an account manager for Pacific Retirement Services, a chain of high-end senior living complexes. They have two children, Gavin (7) and Elise (6). They are both busy finding their niche in life. David's family wins the prize for being furthest from Iowa. We keep trying to get them out of Oregon, into a slower paced Iowa. We have had little luck as of yet.

Both Doris's parents and my parents lived in relatively small houses. The many family reunions they hosted were always crowded. They had people eating in two rooms rather than one. Seating space around the main family table was always limited. It was a challenge playing cards, or watching the Thanksgiving football game in the afternoon. Noise was a factor at my parents' house.

About 12 years ago, Doris and I bought a bigger house to accommodate the large family reunions we anticipated. Since then, we have had all our boys and their families at our our house, together, two times. Distance and busyness have a way of foiling our togetherness efforts. On the other hand, the current locations of these families guarantee Doris and I will travel often to some interesting places. We do enjoy the travel, and seeing each family in their homes and communities.

Marc's Family

Front row (left to right) – Kamryn and Alex
Back row (left to right) – Kelley and Marc

Dan's Family

Left to right – Mari, Elikai, Kolbe, and Dan

David's Family

Front row (left to right) – Gavin and Elise
Back row (left to right) – David and Tanya

Chapter 38

I Finally Enjoy Reading, Writing, and Speaking

Once upon a time I hated everything about reading, and the time it took away from the fun things of life, like playing ball and riding bicycles. Obviously, it follows that I hated writing and speaking. Every report or term paper I wrote was written to the minimum standard. A three-page paper was three pages long. I had nothing extra to add. No doubt there was a lot of fluff in there to get the required three pages.

As far as speaking, I had no confidence whatsoever. Just getting up and introducing myself in a group would cause me to blush and break out in a cold sweat. In college, I took Speech in the summer because summer sessions were only eight weeks long. I did poorly. I received a 'D' for my lackluster efforts. I had little to say and I hated getting up in front of people to say it.

My new faith has given me something important to talk about. I can teach lessons from the Bible and preach sermons, because I know my resource is good. Jesus, my ultimate authority, is pulling for me. He sent me to my world, to share my faith.

I now enjoy reading and learning. I enjoy teaching a good, logical lesson. I look forward to preaching when someone needs a stand-in preacher. I enjoy it because I am sharing Jesus, and how He has changed my life. The Bible has so many lessons. There is no way to run out of material.

Chapter 39

What Will I Be When I Grow Up?

Since I retired from the Rock Island Arsenal in 2006, I have finished our basement. I have had part-time jobs with the Red Cross, Marketplace Chaplains, Morning Star Academy, and Milestones (like meals-on-wheels). Right now I hope to add aspiring author to my resume. Writing these memoirs has been a joy.

I have come to the conclusion that I am not a very good retiree, as I like to be active. I like to have a mental 'to do' list. I like to have a reason to get out of bed each morning.

I was able to experience all my grandparents' love, and attend their funerals. I was able to honor my parents in their aging years, to express my love to them, and to be close at their passing.

Marvin and I got the privilege, with Dad's help, of designing the lovely new tombstone that now marks Mom's and Dad's gravesite just outside the old Brethren Church near Panora, Iowa. This is the church they attended when they were first married. Mom and Dad had purchased a small tombstone years earlier and it was possible for us to replace it with a much nicer tombstone.

My 40 years of teaching adult Sunday school classes have been rewarding. As all teachers know, it is the teacher that learns the most. All the people I have been closest to in later years have come from these classes, or other shared ministries.

One of my part-time jobs listed above was as a Marketplace Chaplain. I provided devotional services and visited with residents of the Bickford Homes in Davenport and Moline. For eight years, I attempted to be a friend to many who were lonely and felt abandoned.

The first nursing home service I presented at Bickford Homes, I apologized for being five minutes late. It makes me laugh to think of that today. Some of them had been there 15 to 20 minutes before I arrived. Others would probably be there 15 to 20 minutes after I left. Some had to wait until help came to get them to their room. The next thing on their schedules was lunch in an hour. What did five minutes late mean to them?

I learned that sermons had to be sermonettes, to keep elderly attentions. Singing old hymns was the highlight of our time together. They knew the words. Those who looked totally out of it, would tap their toes to the music. Those old hymns put them in touch with their old church family, where they had been Sunday school teachers, choir members, and nursery workers. We closed each service by saying the Lord's Prayer together. Most knew the words.

Some of the nicest people you could want to meet were in those facilities. Two of the most hateful people I have ever met were there also. The lesson I take from that is as we age, we are the product of the decisions we have made over our lifetimes. If you love people when you're young, you will probably love them as you age. If you were judgmental and hateful, the decisions you made will ruin your old age too. The Bible says you will reap what you sow, in this world and in the world to come.

After 70 years of life, I have decided my goal now is to be a faithful husband, and a loving father to my three sons and their families. I would like to be known as a good Christian man. I want to be a faithful friend to those who have traveled this road beside me. I have a strong desire to have no hard feelings toward anyone, and to the best of my ability, leave no one upset with me. I pray that I have done that.

Even more, and ultimately, I want to hear Jesus say, "Well done, good and faithful servant." If I hear those words, everything else will be just fine.

Chapter 40

Closing Thoughts

This book has truly been a labor of love. Each morning, during the writing period, I woke up early with a new thought or chapter to add. Hopefully you enjoyed what you read and learned a thing or two along the way. Feel free to quote or pass along any wisdom that you find worthy of sharing.

If you have a question, or would like to reminisce, feel free to contact me. I would be honored to correspond with you. My e-mail address is woodfamily5@msn.com. My cell phone number is (563) 271-3006. My mailing address is 3536 Raleigh Avenue, Bettendorf, Iowa, 52722.

In closing, I will put my name where Billy Graham put his in this statement, "Some day you will read or hear that Keith Wood is dead. Don't you believe a word of it. I shall be more alive than I am now. I will just have changed my new address. I will have gone into the presence of God."

My favorite reading when a friend leaves, is 'Gone From My Sight' by Henry Van Dyke.

> I am standing upon the seashore. A ship, at my side,
> spreads her white sails to the moving breeze and starts
> for the blue ocean. She is an object of beauty and strength.

I stand and watch her until, at length, she hangs like a speck
of white cloud just where the sea and sky
come to mingle with each other.

Then someone at my side says. "There, she is gone."

Gone where?

Gone from my sight. That is all. She is just as large in mast,
hull and spar as she was when she left my side.
And, she is just as able to bear her load of
living freight to her desired port.
Her diminished size is in me – not in her.

And, just at the moment when someone says, "There, she is gone,"
there are other eyes watching her coming, and other voices
ready to take up the glad shout, "Here she comes!"
And that is dying...

I will close with this paraphrase of a C. S. Lewis quote,
"Christians never have to say goodbye for the last time." Thanks
for spending this time with me.

Appendix

Notes From Immediate Family Members

A Few Thoughts from Doris

I will write just a few thoughts about my life as Keith's wife. I came to a very quick realization early in our marriage that Keith's activity level was at a whole different level than mine. We were both teachers our first three years of knowing each other. When I finished a day at school with kids, I was usually ready to collapse into my easy chair and relax in the evening. Keith also said he was tired but his response was usually something like, "I'm really tired too. You want to go play some tennis?" He still often responds similarly. If he's tired he usually feels a need to get up and move, go outside for a walk or a long bike ride, or do some gardening. My response is to to sit and read!!

As I read Keith's memoirs, I again am reminded how much our oldest son, Marcus, was like his dad growing up. Both were a bit on the hyperactive side!! I've heard from both Keith and his brothers how Keith was always trying to get a ball game going. Marc also was always trying to get his brothers outside to play. Kcith always enjoyed coaching and Marc also followed him into coaching. In fact, all 3 of our sons coached at the college level for a while. Marc has now coached college women's soccer for 18 years and it is truly his passion. Keith enjoys hearing about all aspects of Marc's coaching.

Because the boys were quite active, the park board programs with our Parks Department saved me during the summer months.

Every weekday afternoon there were supervised programs at our park across the street. The boys watched carefully each day for the college students that ran the program to arrive and then they were out the door. They played games all afternoon. I seldomly had to come up with activities to entertain them during the summer!! The hard part was getting them to slow down long enough to read some books during the summer!

We didn't take many trips just for fun. Many of our trips were for soccer tournaments. With all the boys playing club soccer, there was usually little time to just go on a family vacation. One year we decided to visit Keith's parents who were living in Indiana. I really looked forward to a weekend without soccer. On our way through Indianapolis, we saw many signs advertising a soccer tournament. The boys begged to stop and watch some games. Of course we gave in, and not only watched some games but bought tournament T-shirts. We also traveled to several major league ball parks. The Milwaukee Brewers were one of their favorites because we always went early and got several baseballs during batting practice that the players hit into the bleachers. We also traveled to Washington D.C. which was a tough trip for Marc especially. Keith was interested in stopping at lots of Civil War sights and the boys were more interested in doing something active. We were at some impressive historical sights and Marc just wanted to stay in the parking lot and dribble his soccer ball. That didn't go over too well with his Dad!!

One of the scarier times in our marriage was Keith's bike accident. He went for one of his long bike rides on a Saturday morning and he didn't come home on time. I had been grocery shopping and didn't know he had crashed on his bike. Thankfully, a jogger came along and called an ambulance. He had broken his arm just below his shoulder and had many bumps and bruises. He also had to have several stitches in his hand. Once his arm healed, he had to have several weeks of physical therapy. He could not do his job delivering meals during that time as it involved heavy lifting. I think he slowed down the pace that he rides just a tiny bit!!

I'm most thankful for the Christian leadership Keith showed to our family. He was faithful at having devotions with the boys at bedtime. There was never any question about where we would be on Sunday morning, if we were in town. I never remember a time when any of the boys complained that they didn't want to go to church. I think having Keith as a male role model in that area was the main reason.

Thank you for the last 46 years, Keith. It's been a fun ride and continues to be.

Brother Carroll's Comments

My name is Carroll Wood, second of five sons. School was hard for me because I was such a slow reader so I never cared for school much. I remember going to country school till 5th grade. We rode one speed bicycles to school and could pump every hill after awhile. We stopped at the four corners east of us and picked up mail on the way home from school. Living on top of the hill, everyone of us put the bikes in the ditch going down the hill sometime.

When we went to Bridgewater to school, I remember having to milk the cows every morning before getting on the school bus a little after 7 o'clock, then again after school. Keith and I milked the cows till he was a senior in high school and I was a junior. Then Dad traded the milk cows for beef cows. I think he didn't want to go back to milking them himself.

We always had chickens around and I can't stand ammonia so cleaning chicken manure was a real trial for me. I never cared much for gathering eggs after getting home from church on Sunday.

I always liked life on the farm but preferred field work to doing chores. I remember even in junior high, I stayed home from school to disk in oats while Mom and Dad seeded them. I was always wanting to drive something.

Dad was a very hard worker who thought he had to be boss to be the head of the household. Honesty was very important to him. I always felt he was trying to be good enough to get into heaven, and to prove to his father that he made the right decision to leave the family farm by Yale. He finally learned later in life, that God's grace through believing in Jesus as your Lord and Savior is a free gift you just have to accept.

Mom was the glue that held the family together. She was always working and serving others. Mom had a strong Christian faith and shared it with everybody. Most people after talking with her would say she was a sweet woman.

I was the only one who had any interest in farming. Dad and Mom were excited about a son farming with them. Looking back, I see Dad was not ready mentally or financially to add a son to the farming operation.

I dated Linda Raasch my senior year in high school. We got engaged at Christmas in 1966. I went to Viet Nam in April of 1967 and we got married on April 28th, 1968 while I was home on leave. Then we moved to Killeen, Texas, for 18 months to finish my army service. Our first child (Angela) was born in Texas. We moved back to Iowa after my service duties were over. I worked at the welding shop in Greenfield. Our 2nd child Jeffrey was born there. We moved to the farm in December of 1971. Jill and Duane were born while we lived on the farm. On April 28th, 2018, Linda and I were married 50 years. We have four children, Angela and husband Jeff Kirby, Jeff and Terri Wood, Jill and Pat Hardy, Duane and Amy Wood and six grandchildren with one grandchild married. We are still farming and very thankful how God has blessed us.

Brother Larry's Comments

My name is Larry Wood. The third son, middle son, of five brothers. I am truly the black sheep of the family. I lived up to my name and perhaps even enjoyed it. Many times it came with consequences. I could not for the life of me understand just because dad made some rule, everyone thought they had to follow it. I took the philosophy if they could make a rule, I could break it.

Needless to say my teenage years were a little challenging for everyone involved. I don't regret for a minute the stands I took but I do regret all the angst and pain I put the folks through. They made far too many trips to school or the sheriff's office because of some stupid thing either I, or my so called friends did. To this day I have no idea how many times I put the car in the ditch. I know I owe a big thank you to all the farmers that pulled me out.

Mom - In my opinion she was a saint. She always talked to dad first, when I got in trouble, so that she could get my punishment reduced. I'm not sure it ever worked but I know she tried on my behalf. I always remember her working. She was cooking, sewing, gardening, or whatever it took for her family to survive. Her family meant everything to her and she would do whatever it took to please us and dad. I truly believe she was the patriot of our family.

Dad - For some reason Dad and I just really didn't get along very well. I wanted to enjoy life, and he just didn't seem to have time for a lot of my foolishness. I know now that he was really just trying to survive and I surely didn't make that any easier. We had many good conversations after Mom was gone, while playing cribbage. I think we both finally understood where the other one was coming from. Perhaps we were both too bull headed, so we just collided a lot.

Brothers - I will forever be known as the wild child by my brothers and for good reasons. Every time I got in trouble, they all got punished. We spent a lot of time picking up rocks, building fence, pitching manure, and a lot of other undesirable jobs that was supposed to help build character or something. It seemed like we were always doing chores. It was my job to gather the eggs, feed and water chickens while my older brothers milked the cows. At one time we had over 1,000 laying hens so it was no small job. We also had to pack one full case of eggs every night. During the winter months I would volunteer to get up in the middle of the night and go check the sows that were having little pigs for Dad. If I did, I didn't have to chore in the mornings. I used to love getting under the heat lamps to get warm and playing with the little pigs. More than once I fell asleep and Dad would come looking for me. I do remember playing lots of baseball games, hunting sparrows with BB guns, and playing cards in the evening. I always loved games, and still do.

Family – I entered the military right out of school. I was stationed in Nuremberg, Germany. Six months after being discharged I married Judy. We have been married 47 years this year. We had

3 children, Sheila, Dallas, & Scott. We have 5 grand children and one great grandchild. Our youngest son was killed in a car accident at the age of 22. After getting married I worked at the Free Press for 24 years, 10 years at a furniture factory, 3 year at Precision Optional, and am currently part-time custodian at O-M school. We have a lot of health issues in our family so we struggle both physically and financially.

Through it all, my faith has grown stronger, and I truly believe God will see me through in good times and bad. I am just beginning to realize all the blessings I have, and how lucky I am to be part of the Wood family.

Brother Dean's Comments

My name is Dean Arthur Wood, the fourth son of Arden and Norma Jean. It is important to have Arthur in there since I am named after Grandpa Wood, and I still have the silver dollar given to me to prove it. Mom told me that when she found out she was pregnant with me, she cried. I was born on January 21, 1952. Even though I was the star of the show I do not recall anything that went on that day. Mom said dad had to put chains on the car before they could go to the hospital. While I was an infant, mom was so thankful I was such a good baby.

By far the most memorable event in my childhood was being plopped, along with Larry, under the water hydrant after we had covered ourselves with manure from the hog lot. I still do not know how sub-zero water could flow through pipes. Obviously, the water temperature had to of been a little warmer. To this day, some 60+ years later, I still shiver just thinking of that episode in my life. Dad said he never saw mom so mad. After washing our manure covered clothes about three times, the stink was still present. Mom finally burned the clothes. Can you imagine how bad those clothes had to of been for mom to burn them?

Not to upscale Larry at all, I feel compelled to add a few details to Larry's driving adventures. If it were a Friday night, the weather less than favorable, and Larry took the car out, Saturday morning dad and I would be on a car rescue. Of all the things that had a tendency to upset dad, retrieving a ditched car was not one of them. Amazingly, Dad just seemed to accept the fact we would have to pull a car home. We had it down to a science. I do recall one instance where Larry outdid himself. He planted a car into a shallow ditch a considerable distance from the traveled road, and it must have frozen to the ground during the night. As much as the tractor screamed and begged for mercy, the car budged not an inch. Fortunately, a man on a road grader came by and saw our problem. I do not think he realized the fight he was to encounter. After about three failed attempts to dislodge the car, I think the maintainer operator decided the car was coming out one way or another. He gave the horses under the hood plenty of feed and released the clutch. I can still see all four of the drive tires just squatting under the tremendous strain being applied to them. The car finally cried "uncle" and came loose. It is hard to believe that everyone and all the equipment came out unscathed.

A very pleasant memory is the fact that dad made a real effort to be at my sporting events. He was moving up and down the sidelined with the line of scrimmage at a football game or sitting in a lawn chair at a baseball game. No matter where he was, coaching and/or refereeing was mandatory. I do not think dad ever lost a game.

Mom was invariably in the kitchen cooking or washing another load of clothes. In the summer she had the added responsibility of tending a huge garden. Although it was a lot of work, I think mom enjoyed gardening. She did not pass that love on to this son. No matter how much effort or how long it took, mom kept the house running.

The greatest gift the folks gave our family was a fear and love of our Lord and Savior Jesus Christ. That same love is being passed on to many kids, grandkids, great grandkids, etc. Thank you Dad and Mom.

Brother Marvin's Random Memories

A. Our old house:

1. The furnace being in the living room and one night it caught fire

2. The tank with fuel oil that sat outside Mom's sewing room

3. Mom hiding our presents in the sewing room underneath the stairs

4. No hot water in the house so Mom heated our bathwater on the stove

5. Mom had some kind of electric wand that she used for awhile to heat the water.
   I am surprised it did not kill one or several of us.

6. Getting out of the bathtub and standing by the furnace to get warm and getting too close to it – a real hot <u>seat</u>!
   I don't remember if I got blisters or not from it.

7. Dean put sand down the stool to see what would happen – Dad was pretty upset as he had to bring in a tractor with a scoop on the front to dig up the pipes north of the house.

8. The TV set – black and white which was hooked up to the antenna so we could get both Des Moines and Omaha stations. Six channels tops I believe.

9. There were 16 families on our party line (8 that we could hear ring and 8 we could not hear). I believe our ring was two longs and two shorts. We finally got down to only four families on our line. We listened to the Walter's boys

talk to their girlfriends. We breathed heavily enough so they would ask each other if the other one was making that noise. Then they would wonder if someone was listening in on them.

10. Packing eggs on the porch and in the cellar when we bought a light to show us if the eggs were bad.
11. There was no heat upstairs, so there were vents in the floor, so that the heat would rise and provide some warmth upstairs.
12. Carroll's room had some screened storage by his bed.
13. The pot that was used as needed at night.

B. Tearing down the old house:

1. We tore the plaster off the upstairs first and then saved the chicken stats so they could be sold to the lumber yard in bundles of 50.
2. Dad pulled the porch away from the house and we had bunked, double beds with no bathroom – for some reason the grass turned white near the door.
3. We pulled nails from the lumber from the old house and from the barn we tore down on the north 40.
4. Since we had no bathroom we took our weekly baths in a metal tub in the barnyard at least some of the time.
5. There was a two-holer in the shed to the north of the house. I do not remember when we tore that tool shed down but it had to be before we put up the new house.
6. The one thing I do remember was that Dad had a sheet of paper with different sizes of nails and that really helped me learn the different types and sizes.
7. Grandpa and Grandma Bancroft lived in the corn crib. Our living room, kitchen, and kitchen table were there

also. The refrigerator shocked me almost every time I opened it.

8. Grandpa made fly catchers out of chicken wire and they really did work.

9. I remember one time Grandpa took me to town and told me I needed to try a pineapple malt (I thought it sounded disgusting but it was really good.)

10. I do not remember where Mom and Dad slept.

11. To this day I regret that I did not learn more about building a house and all its parts but it was my way of rebelling – Dad could make me work but I did not have to pay any attention. That was a decision that has cost me a lot of money over the years!

12. I so remember Jim Sullivan laying the blocks for our basement. I carried a lot of blocks to him so he could lay them faster which, I guess, helped save money.

13. It seems a lot of what we did was to save money, such as Mom burying the tongue and other disgusting parts of our butchered cows in other dishes.

14. Some neighbors helped to put up the walls and the rafters. Dad taught us to put them into place upside down and flip them over when we were ready to put them in permanently. I remembered that trick when I helped a church member put his wall and rafters up. Everyone was amazed at how well it worked.

15. We slept in the basement of the new house for an extended period of time while the main floor was being built.

16. I think I begged Mom and Dad into letting me sleep upstairs before it was ready one time. The house had electric heat so if you were really cold there was almost

no place to go to get warm. It also took a long time for the house to warm up if we left for any amount of time.

C. Ballgames in the barnyard, lot, north of the barn, in the pasture east of the well, and at Vacation Bible School
   1. Keith was always trying to get some kind of ballgame going. We weren't very good but we <u>were</u> competitive. No one liked losing to anyone else under any circumstances. (note – see cards!)
   2. After we shelled corn and put the cobs in the lot in front of the barn, I remember playing home run derby – hitting cobs from one side over the east fence of the lot.
   3. We played cross out with a rubber ball in the barnyard. Home plate was the barn, first was where the 2 doors met on the corn crib, second was on the east side of the house, third was about the middle of the driveway.
   4. I was left handed, as was Grandpa (Arthur) Wood. Mom and Dad never bought me a left handed glove so I either learned to play right handed or not play at all.
   5. To this day, I only eat, play pool and ping pong left handed. Sorry, not true, I hammer nails left handed and Dad never got over the fact that I could not nail very well.
   6. Steve Conley and Curtis Brown were often in our games as well.
   7. Football games were tackle with no pads. I think this made me a good linebacker in high school because I learned every way to tackle without overpowering anybody. Everyone was at least 2 years older than me.
   8. One of my fondest memories was when we were playing football in a mass of people in Bridgewater and a lot of

Keith's friends were playing. I told Keith to pass me the football, as no one was even guarding me. I caught it and scored a touchdown.

9. Carroll welded us a rim that we fastened to a back board on the corn crib for our basketball games.

10. We usually played with winter clothes on such as coveralls and boots. I think it was closer to gym slaughter than basketball and a lot of unusual shots were taken. Some of them went in on occasion.

11. At the time, I think the baseball games at Vacation Bible School were more important to us than the lessons we learned. Our teachers taught us a lot but it was important to be the winning team during the breaks.

12. We had to be called in several times before we actually came in there at Highland Church.

13. When Dean and I (probably Larry also, but I'm not sure) played under Coach Bob Daugherty, Dad was pretty vocal. I was pretty good at tuning Dad out when he hollered at us.

14. When I coached baseball at Glidden-Ralston we played a game against Coach Daugherty's Dunlap team. He said, "It didn't seem like a real game without your Dad giving me "heck" the whole game." I was upset that my team lost to him though.

D. Food:

1. I always loved Mom's fried dough bread, red jello with bananas in it, and cinnamon rolls.

2. I never liked steak all that much because, as I found out later, Mom was not about to see blood running out of her meat. Perhaps that was why our meat was so dry and

why to this day I put ketchup, mustard, and steak sauce on almost everything.

3. Mom was very good at using everything we had if it would help to feed the family including adding water to the soup to make it go farther.

4. I remember thinking if you want seconds you had to eat firsts really fast or there was nothing left.

5. Dad used to drink humongous amounts of milk.

6. There always seemed to be a thick layer of cream on the milk in the pitcher.

7. Mom's gardens seemed to be very large. Would I be wrong to say they were at least and acre in size. Everything seemed to grow so well which meant an awful lot of work harvesting tomatoes, sweet corn, beans, peas, etc. It also meant a lot of canning and she had that operation down to a science. The work included silking, cutting the corn off the cobs, snapping beans, cutting tomatoes, jars, lids, and the pressure cooker going full force.

8. The orchard north of the house provided plenty of fruit especially apples, pears, and cherries. I was always surprised at how much they let us eat when picking the fruit.

E. And Now to Cards;

1. Playing cards was always a time to look forward to in the family.

2. If ever there was a cut throat competitiveness it was every hand ever played.

3. Whoa be unto the individual who made a dumb move, even if it was Mom.

4. You could expect to be called several derisive terms if you played the wrong card or went set. In 10-point pitch the bid never seemed to be less than seven.

5. I always enjoyed playing with Larry as he continually overbid his hand and most times he seemed to win those hands. I could never figure out how he did it. It seemed like he would bid 7 before he even looked at his cards.

6. We used to play pinochle a lot. There was one game where it seemed Dad had almost all the cards in one suit. After the hand was over we figured out he had a double run (one of the best hands you can get) and he completely missed it. As you might imagine, we said nothing out of respect for our father. (WRONG!!!)

7. Mom's club would have Saturday night card parties every so often and Hump Conley was a wild bidder like Larry. He seemed to make his bids also.

8. A bowl of popcorn was necessary for playing cards and usually it was several bowls made on the stove in Mom's skillet.

9. I remember playing with Dennis Bower, the Lents brothers, Russell and Ron (Mumbles) Mangels, JC McCall, and anyone else with thick enough skin to join us. Our wives never seem/seemed to want to enjoy our festivities and even had the audacity to say we were too loud, can you believe that?!?

10. We would play cards sometimes when the Wood family uncles and aunts got together. I think they felt we were the most competitive family.

11. It is hard to believe this, but I feel like it was our family's way of saying, "I love you" to each other.

12. There was always lots of news, events, and gossip passed along during cards.

F. Farm work:
1. I personally did not like being on the farm, but, I must admit that it taught me a lot about hard work, perseverance, and discipline that I needed to know.
2. I always figured if you could pitch a load of manure onto the manure spreader there were few legal jobs beneath your dignity.
3. Many Saturdays were spent cleaning out the chicken houses, pig lots, and cattle lots. It was fun to take the manure spreader out and watching the beaters make the manure fly up in the air and land on the fields.
4. There was one time I forgot which way the wind was blowing, I turned the tractor and manure spreader around, and I was covered by the "smell of money".
5. We had different tractors over time but I mainly remember our Allis-Chalmers WD and, my favorite was the WD 45. I really liked Hump's D17 with the wide front end.
6. Our farm was small, only 120-acres. I think it was originally 80-acres until Dad and Mom bought 40-acres from Jack Brown.
7. I remember tearing down that barn for the wood to be used in the new house.
8. We hired out to the neighbors a lot to make hay. I started at Forey Bassett's to drive a tractor. I made $8.00 for 8 hours work when I was 8 years old.

Son Marc's Comments

Growing up in the Wood Family

I had a dream to be a part of great TEAM. I did not realize at the time, I was already surrounded by a great TEAM. My family was an incredible TEAM. My parents, Keith and Doris Wood were the most supportive parents that anyone could ask for. They prayed for me before I was born and they covered my life in prayer. They taught their three boys, by example, to love the Lord and to love our family. My dad grew up as a farmer in Iowa and taught us a farmer's work ethic. The way Dad lived his values was an inspiration to our entire family. Dad, I am incredibly proud to be your son.

My mom mostly taught me sacrifice. Mom sacrificed for our family. She gave everything to her family and we all noticed. Our Mom clearly saw one of her important roles in life was to raise her children. I have memories of coming home late for curfew as a teenager. Mom was always up and ready for the fight. I always fought back about how the curfew was ridiculous. My younger brother Dan chose a different strategy. He was also late. He chose to take the lecture and then would ask, "Are you done?" Our youngest brother, Dave, mostly followed the rules.

My parents fought the good fight and raised their 3 boys according to the Bible. Man we were conservative. I could not go to PG-13 movies because they were too vulgar. As an adult I can see the wisdom in these decisions. As a kid it felt like we were really missing out. My Mom and Dad may not be famous but they are great people. They each taught me many things and put me on a path for life.

I shared a love for sports with my brothers Dan and David Wood. It started with baseball and wrestling. These two sports were the sports that Dad taught us. They were the sports that he knew. Baseball and wrestling probably make sense growing up in Iowa. The strongest story that emerges was Dan's dominance in baseball. We kept stats and Dan's batting average was around .800 with many home runs, RBI's and multiple no hitters. Dan was throwing a curve ball at age 10 that was pretty potent. Dad coached the team. Dave was the bat boy. Theo Epstein had nothing on Keith Wood. So Dan's baseball team brought home a number of trophies.

The wrestling story we enjoy telling is Dave's debut/only wrestling match of his life. Dave was starting young because he was the youngest brother. At the youngest age they take the 5 year olds and pair them up by size. You wrestle one kid for 3 or 4 minutes then they move you along and you wrestle another kid. You wrestle 3 or 4 kids then every kid gets a medal. We are pretty certain that in Dave's 5 year old match up he was paired with Cael Sanderson. Dave was pinned about 10 times in a 2 minute window and was quickly crying. We would dust him off and get him back out on the mat against his little dominating opponent. After one match Dave would not go wrestle any of the other kids. We tried to assure him that if he would take an attempt at some of the other opponents it would be better. But Dave had enough. Dave retired with one wrestling match and a medal.

At age 12, I focused all of my energy on soccer. Shortly after Dan & Dave joined me, and we were out of the sports that Dad knew and could teach. Soccer was just much more fun than baseball or wrestling. I remember a long fight to join the Bettendorf Soccer Association (BSA). My parents did not want to travel and pay the expenses, and games would often require missing church on Sunday. We reached the compromise that if a game took place on Sunday morning we would skip it and go to church in whatever town the game was located. I was embarrassed by this fact as a kid but love this story today. No other kids on any of our teams ever had to miss a game for church. Dad was going to live his priorities, no matter how much we were kicking and screaming.

When we made the decision to join BSA Dad and I went on a jog to the Schara's house to pay our dues. We fell in love with the game and we shared it together. When we made the state Olympic Development Program team my parents would not pay the fee. I detassled corn to pay for ODP events. I think Dan did the same. Detassling was solid work. I think my parents went soft by the time Dave was going through and paid the way for Dave. I learned the value of a dollar. The financial lessons learned have served our family well.

Dan and Dave both won state championships in club soccer and in high school soccer. In Dave's senior year his club team won the state championship. At the time I was coaching at University of the Cumberlands in Kentucky. Over the summer the coaching staff that led them to the state title gave me the honor of coaching the team in Regional Championships in the summer. The regional competition was the state champions from the 14 Midwest states. The regionals would be the last weekend of soccer for one of the truly great BSA teams. The weekend started great tying Vardar out of Michigan 1-1. Michigan went on to win the regional and advanced to nationals as one of the best 4 teams in the country. We lost the last two games decisively and we were extremely disappointed. Dave was a great player and we found players better than us. I was aspiring to be a coach and I had been out coached.

On the drive home from regionals we stopped at Grandpa Wood's house in Des Moines. He greeted us by saying, "So you stubbed your toe! I guess you are not as good as you thought you were!" Grandpa was talking trash like we were playing a game of cards. Grandpa's infamous trash talking was not going to be slowed by the fact that this really meant a lot to us. Grandpa's joking somehow took the sting out of the losses. The lesson seemed to be to not take yourself too seriously. Enjoy your work. Sometime you will fall down but get up and go again.

Watching Mom and Dad as grandparents has given me something to really aspire to. At age 43 my energy is sometimes lacking as a parent. My kids energy seems to outlast my energy every night at bedtime. When my parents visit I am so impressed with the amount of energy they invest into Kamryn and Alex. Kam and Alex love Grandma and Grandpa.

Kamryn's Comments

Hello! I'm Kamryn Wood. I'm Keith's oldest grandchild. I am 10 years old. I have strawberry blond hair. I have hazel\green eyes. Freckles almost cover my face and arms. You won't catch me wearing fancy outfits very often. It's always a T-shirt and shorts out here in Abilene, Texas!

I LOVE ANIMALS! They are fascinating and CUTE creatures. I already have a hamster and a dog. My dog's name is Leo. Leo is 2 years old. He is the cutest dog I HAVE EVER SEEN! Humphrey is my hamster. My mom got him for me as an "early Christmas present."

I'll also have to have a job besides farming when I grow up! I'll be a zookeeper, artist, and author! That might sound impossible, but trust me, I CAN DO IT! I have an amazing potential. I can do hard things. I am never alone. I DREAM BIG! Believe in yourself! I do!

Alexander Wood is my brother. He is 6 years old. I admit, he is one of the few people who can make me TRULY mad. He is EXCEPTIONAL at making me mad. In fact, I think he could go to college right now, and get a degree on making me mad! At the times he's not being little Mr. Whiny Pants, we get along quite well. We play all sorts of little games! We have many toys and games to play with! We are the best of friends! (Sometimes.)

I love my mom. She is an amazing person. She is the BEST! She tries to make our lives as wonderful and "tear free" as possible! (Get it? Tear free! Like on soap bottles! Ha, ha!) My mom and I go lots of fun places like Fossil Rim, museums, downtown, and more! We play all day in the summertime! She tries to get jobs where she can be with us as much as possible!

Daddy is SOOOOOOO fun! He would play with us all day if it weren't for old age! He just turned 43 and we're starting to see gray hairs. Yet, my dad will never be truly old, for his personality is that of an energetic child! He plays with us as much as possible. He is always trying to make us happy! He is a soccer coach. He has traveled much of the world! Many of his players have babysat Alex and I. My favorites are Caitlin, Kyleigh, Kaleigh, and Morgan. Though my dad is often away, he still finds ways to be with us, and keep us happy.

I have 2 sets of grandmas and grandpas. Grandma and Grandpa Wood are 2 very generous people. They visit about twice a year (not counting holidays) and every time they bring us some sort of gift. They use the time they have with us wisely, making sure to get just enough fun in. Though old age is starting to show, they make the best of their time. They are great people! Thanks Grandma and Grandpa!

My mom's mom and dad are Grandma and Grandpa T. (T. stands for Tragesser) They are divorced. Grandpa married a nice lady named Zina. They now live in North Carolina. Grandma T. lives in Illinois, by my Aunt Meghan and her daughters and son, who live in St. Louis, Missouri. Grandma T. is also very nice. I have visited her many times, and we always make wonderful memories! I have amazing grandparents!

I also have many great aunts and uncles! Most of my aunts are very kind and loving people. A few are active and playful people! My uncles are all funny people. They are always making me laugh! Some of them are not only funny, but very nice and helping. All my aunts and uncles are exceptional people.

I have many cousins. All are very loving. My cousins are probably the relatives I'm closest to. I love them very much. Taylor (Tay Tay) is a cousin I've known since I was a baby. She is 14 now. She is still one of my favorite and most memorable relatives I've known. Kolbe is an adorable little cousin of mine. She is the sweetest and cutest little girl I've seen. I wish we could live closer so that I could see her more often. Same goes for Lily. She is an adorable and awesome young girl. Caleb is Lily's brother. He is a nice boy. He will grow up to be a kind (and strong) young man. Kolbe's brother's name is Elikai. He is a growing boy. He will grow up to be a strong and healthy young man. Brook is another one of my cousins. She's much older than me, about Tay Tay's age. She is very fun and energetic. Owen and Quin are Taylor's little brother and sister. They are adorable! Owen just turned 3! Quin has the cutest curly hair!

What is it like to be part of the Wood family? My mom, my dad, my brother, and me go to church every Sunday. We are Christians. I love my family. I love God. I am loved. I am taught what is right and wrong. I try to stay on the path of Christ. I'm working on a good relationship with my brother. My family is full of love.

I have a VERY extended family. It goes on FOREVER! I love them all. Most, or maybe even all of us know God. We believe in Him. We are all very kind people. A few words that describe us are brave, bold, funny, helpful, smart, and AWESOMELY AMAZING!

I hope you enjoyed learning about me, my family, and my life. Never stop reading! Never stop learning!

Alex's comments

My name is Alexander Marcus Wood. I am 6 years old. I will be going to school full-time this fall. I am kind of shy, but I really enjoy being the center of attention with my own family. I like to snuggle with my Mom. I like Mom to read to me at bedtime. I like having sleep-overs with my family. I like to wrestle with Dad. Kamryn and I play Alexville and Kamrynville. It is a lot of fun pretending.

I really like chocolate ice cream. I like chicken fingers and chicken nuggets (with lots of ketchup), especially from Chick-fil-A. I enjoy riding my bike and jumping on the trampoline at home. While my preference is to stay home in my pajamas, I enjoy most activities once I get there.

Grandpa keeps trying to put words in my mouth. He says I am going to have to pick it up if I am going to be a Wood boy. Actually I am not sure the standard is nearly as high as Grandpa thinks it is. Even so, I will do my best.

About the Author

Keith Wood is a retired school teacher, accountant, and part-time assisted living chaplain. He has a BA in business education from the University of Northern Iowa in 1968, a BS in Christian Ministry from Iowa Christian College in 1976, and an MBA from St. Ambrose University in 2000.

He lives in Bettendorf, Iowa with his wife Doris. Giving out the general location of Bettendorf, he likes to tell people, "If you can picture Iowa with a nose, Bettendorf is where you would use a Kleenex."

They raised three boys, who now live too many miles from their Iowa roots, raising families of their own. Keith's 46 years of family life, work life, and church life have been the source of many experiences. Experiences that added to the early lessons of an Iowa farm boy. The reminiscing here is part of his continuous search for meaning throughout his 72 years of life.

Printed in the United States
By Bookmasters